Curiosities

POETS ON POETRY

David Lehman, General Editor
Donald Hall, Founding Editor

New titles

John Koethe, *Poetry at One Remove*
Yusef Komunyakaa, *Blue Notes*
Alicia Suskin Ostriker, *Dancing at the Devil's Party*

Recently published

Thom Gunn, *The Occasions of Poetry*
Edward Hirsch, *Responsive Reading*
John Hollander, *The Poetry of Everyday Life*
Philip Larkin, *Required Writing*
Geoffrey O'Brien, *Bardic Deadlines*
James Tate, *The Route as Briefed*

Also available are collections by

A. R. Ammons, Robert Bly, Philip Booth, Marianne Boruch,
Hayden Carruth, Fred Chappell, Amy Clampitt, Tom Clark,
Douglas Crase, Robert Creeley, Donald Davie, Peter Davison,
Tess Gallagher, Suzanne Gardinier, Allen Grossman, Thom Gunn,
John Haines, Donald Hall, Joy Harjo, Robert Hayden,
Daniel Hoffman, Jonathan Holden, Andrew Hudgins,
Josephine Jacobsen, Weldon Kees, Galway Kinnell, Mary Kinzie,
Kenneth Koch, Richard Kostelanetz, Maxine Kumin,
Martin Lammon (editor), David Lehman, Philip Levine,
John Logan, William Logan, William Matthews, William Meredith,
Jane Miller, Carol Muske, John Frederick Nims, Gregory Orr,
Marge Piercy, Anne Sexton, Charles Simic, Louis Simpson,
William Stafford, Anne Stevenson, May Swenson,
Richard Tillinghast, Diane Wakoski, C. K. Williams,
Alan Williamson, Charles Wright, and James Wright

William Matthews

Curiosities

Ann Arbor
The University of Michigan Press

Library of Congress Cataloging-in-Publication Data

Matthews, William, 1942–
  Curiosities / William Matthews.
        p.   cm. — (Poets on poetry)
    ISBN 0-472-09388-6 (alk. paper) — ISBN 0-472-06388-X
(pbk. : alk. paper)
    I. Title.   II. Series.
PS3563.A855C8 1989
814'.54—dc20   89-5127
                                                        CIP

For Robert Morgan

Thinking is more interesting than knowing,
but less interesting than looking.

—Goethe

Preface

The introductory note apologizing for a collection of incidental, assigned, or occasional pieces is by now a rhetorical commonplace. It's also a heap on which I'd rather place no straw.

"Remarks are not literature," Gertrude Stein said icily, and hers has all the more force for her avid pursuit of remarks in her salons and of literature at her desk.

But these are essays, not remarks.

"One feels that what holds one's attention might hold the attention of others," wrote Marianne Moore. Exactly.

I'm grateful to the editors of all the periodicals and books in which these pieces first appeared, but especially to Wayne Dodd and Syd Lea for their perceptive suggestions and support.

Acknowledgments

Many of the essays in this book have been previously published:

"Dull Subjects," "Richard Hugo and Detective Fiction," "Dishonesty and Bad Manners," and "Ignorance" first appeared in the *New England Review & Bread Loaf Quarterly.*

"Lines," "On Stanley Plumly's *Summer Celestial,*" "The Continuity of James Wright's Poems," and "Wagoner, Hugo, and Levine" first appeared in the *Ohio Review.*

"Anita O'Day and I" first appeared in *Brushes with Greatness,* edited by Russell Banks, Michael Ondaatje, and David Young (Toronto: Coach House Press, 1989). Reprinted by permission.

"Merida, 1969" first appeared in *Ecstatic Occasions, Expedient Forms,* edited by David Lehman (New York: Macmillan, 1987).

"Cameo Roles" first appeared in the *Wallace Stevens Journal.*

"Horatian Hecht" first appeared in *The Burden of Formality,* edited by Sydney Lea (University of Georgia Press, 1989). Reprinted by permission.

"Moving Around" first appeared in *American Poets in 1976,* edited by William Heyen (New York: Bobbs-Merrill, 1976).

"On the Tennis Court at Night" first appeared in *On the Poetry of Galway Kinnell: The Wages of Dying,* edited by Howard Nelson (Ann Arbor: University of Michigan Press, 1987).

"Personal and Impersonal" first appeared in the *Seattle Review.*

"Billie Holiday and Lester Young" first appeared in the *Missouri Review.*

"Travel" first appeared in *Antaeus.*

"A Poet's Alphabet" first appeared in the *Black Warrior Review.*

Every effort has been made to trace the ownership of all copyrighted material and to obtain permission for its use.

Contents

Long Shadows

*Summer afternoon—summer
afternoon; to me those have
always been the two most
beautiful words in the English
language.*

—Henry James

I'd won a month's work at the Rockefeller Foundation's Villa
Serbelloni, occupying the fifty most beautiful and command-
ing acres of the promontory at Bellagio, and by the time I got
there, via Rome and Sicily and Verona and Milan, my work
was not only to write but also to repair a broken heart, and to
fight, while I mended, the despair of having taken on such a
familiar job all too often and each time with the optimistic
notion that this time I'd get it right. "All this buttoning and
unbuttoning," reads the entirety of an anonymous eighteenth
century suicide note, but if it had overshot its desperate brev-
ity it might have gone on to say, "and now my work is done."

Getting work done would be a disarming preoccupation at
the Villa. The artists there would be building with the mixed
feelings native to the metaphor of their "bodies of work,"
which grow suppler as their actual bodies stiffen and creak.
"If I had the use of my body," Beckett has one of his charac-
ters cry out, "I'd hurl it out the window."

I felt crucially better than that, though sometimes crucial
isn't much, and twisted into the back of the limousine the Villa
had sent to my hotel in Milan.

What did I know about Bellagio? There's a single glacially
scooped lake whose stark, cold waters run south from the

Alps and get divided by the promontory: the western branch is Lake Como and the eastern branch Lake Lecco.

What did I know about the Villa? The Rockefeller Foundation brings 165 of us a year to work and be fed and housed in style for up to a month. The gardens at the Villa are open twice a day for guided tours, but otherwise the property is closed to the public.

"You'll love it," friends who'd been there told me. "Lucky duck," friends who hadn't quacked. "What will you bring me from Italy?" I could hear a sleepy, hopeful voice asking. But whose? Sweet baby Jesus, it was mine.

✖

Pliny the Younger had two villas in the vicinity, and one may well have been on the current site of the Villa Serbelloni. "It enjoys," he wrote, "a broad view of the lake, which the ridge on which it stands divides in two."

The descent to town is steep. M. has counted 283 stairsteps. In the village itself most of the streets are stone staircases connecting the one street wide enough for cars to the lakefront.

I love, as I do in any new place, my first orientation trip to town. I find the post office, a stationery shop, a wine shop, and an outdoor café where I can sit with a cappucino and watch the late afternoon strollers. I walk every street, even and especially the tiny Via Musica, some twenty yards long and half of that under a fat arch. As I locate my various goals, I go into each for a small purchase and launch a rote flurry of commercial Italian, with its ritual finale.

"*Grazie.*"

"*Prego.*"

I climb back from my exploratory visit with aching calves.

✖

At breakfast R.D. reports a dream about a wrestling match. One of the contestants has been born with a hunchback but by dint of hard work has got rid of it. Suddenly, in midmatch, it pops up again.

Also, there's talk of an expedition to Verona to see *La Gioconda* sung at the Arena. Suddenly my unfurling morning imagination is at work on an outline for an opera libretto, *Il Gobbo* (The Hunchback).

But then we already have *Rigoletto*, I realize. Never mind; I'll just raise the ante. My opera will be called *Tredice Gobbi* (Thirteen Hunchbacks), its title stolen from the name of a restaurant in Florence.

I imagine the second act ballet, both tender and grotesque, in which the spiraled thirteen descend from their dormitory to ready themselves for the day's contumely. They rub each other's humps for luck. They shoulder their capes and swirl into a world all too thoughtlessly ready to treat them as freaks. Franco, the tenor, lingers for an aching aria about his love for La Diretta, whose exemplary posture and penchant for romance at short notice make her cruelly inaccessible to him. . . .

✖

Of course there's no television at the Villa. The Italian papers arrive on the day of release, and the French, German, and Swiss papers and the *International Herald Tribune* sometimes that day and sometimes the next.

In any case it's Sunday. A few shops will open anyway; Bellagio is a tourist town and summer is high season.

"Everyone is bored on Sundays," runs the French proverb. Of course there's no mail, though in any case it takes two weeks or more to get an airmail letter from Bellagio to the States or vice versa.

The stimuli just don't come in. Even the industrious, affluent Milanese who drive to the lakes for summer weekends seem drowsy; soon they'll drive back. A hornet wafts in and out the open window of my studio, building a nest against one side of the fireplace. Sundays you have to make do with what's at hand.

✖

After Pliny the Younger, the Villa Serbelloni property disappears from record for a thousand years. In the Middle Ages, because of the promontory's strategic command of two lakes, it was a pawn in the Guelf and Ghibelline struggles. In 1369 the Viscontis had the buildings razed rather than meet the expenses to defend them. In the next century the property "came into the hands of the Sforzas," dukes of Milan. Sale was not the most prominent method of real estate transfer in those years, but the Sforzas were powerful enough to secure the property and sell it to Marchesino Stanga in 1489. In the sixteenth century the property was owned by Count (later Cardinal) Francesco Sfondrati of Milan. He built a great house there and planted gardens on the stony upper slopes of the promontory. His grandson built a monastery for some Milanese Capuchin Brothers; the building is decrepit but standing today. He also built a tower by the Lecco shore and spent his life peacefully improving the estate. Then it was transferred to another Milanese, Alessandro Serbelloni, in 1788.

In 1855 the Serbellonis sold the property to a Swiss hotelier, and in 1928 Ella Walker, heiress to the Hiram Walker fortune, bought the property for a residence. The Grand Hotel Villa Serbelloni, on Bellagio's lakefront, got detached in that transaction and is still in splendid, anachronistic, and slightly musty business today.

Walker's third marriage was to the Duke of Duino, head of the Italian branch of the Thurn and Taxis family. All her marriages were childless, and just before she died in 1959, at the age of eighty-four, she willed the property to the Rockefeller Foundation.

You can show up for breakfast anytime from 7:30 to 9:00. Freshly made rolls have been driven up from a bakery in the village (the driver makes a gravel-spewing turn at high speed just under the window of my bedroom, and thus serves as my alarm clock), and there's sweet butter and jam, and fresh fruit, picked for the most part from trees on the property. There's juice and coffee and cereal. The lake is already exhaling haze. The Villa's sprinkler system twitters. Across Lake Lecco cars and trucks drone toward Switzerland through tunnels cut in the mountainsides where the cliffs rake down so steeply there was no room to grade a lakeside road. Now and then you can hear a truck downshift, and then the sound is sucked into a tunnel.

After breakfast we'll head for our studios. M.C., the composer, has a piano in his, and one is set up to be used by a painter, but most of them are like mine: A desk, a typing table, a comfortable desk chair, and a good armchair for reading in. There's a good electric typewriter, though of course these days many residents bring computers or rent them here. There's a dictionary, an encyclopedia (*Britannica*, fifteenth edition), a small pile of office supplies.

Aperitivi at 12:30 and lunch at 1:00, and then back to the studios.

This is the day's long prospect, for drinks are at 7:30 and dinner at 8:00. There are many distractions. You can go to Como and shop for silk. Several of the lakeside villages are beautiful and easily reached by ferry. Bergamo, particularly the old town, rewards an ambling day's visit. You can walk down to Bellagio and loiter and watch people drink cappucino and loiter some more and watch. You can swim in Lake Lecco or take the Villa's rowboat out, play on the Villa's tennis court, or just wander around the Villa's fifty acres.

When will you next be in Italy? It would be folly not to forge some excursions, to soak in leisure and beauty. The office supplies and typewriter will wait, and wait they do. They'll wait for the Faulkner scholar who succeeds you and the Polish historian who follows her and then for the musicologist from Rangoon.

"I can't even bear to think about group therapy," complained a psychoanalyst-in-training I know; she had to put in a certain number of hours of it to pass to the next stage of her training. "Those fifteen chairs," she shivered, "those fifteen boxes of tissue paper. . . ." The office supplies and typewriter wait for you like that.

A cicada is sawing away in the oak outside your studio. It's 4:37, hot and limply muggy. Two glasses of Pinot Grigio with the tagliolini at lunch didn't seem much at the time, but now you too are limply muggy. While you were at lunch the maid came to empty your studio wastebasket and close the window. You fling it open again: 4:39.

And yet there are afternoons the work unrolls before you the way the ground seems to rise to meet your feet on a good walk. When you show up at 7:30 for drinks someone will ask politely, "How did it go?"

After a good afternoon, I play it close to the vest. "Not bad," I say, and then to the waiter, "Campari and orange juice, please." If I've had a terrific afternoon, I order it in Italian. If I've had a long, stupid afternoon, I say "Fine, just fine." Work is the core of privacy here. "Never to lie is to have no lock to your door," wrote Elizabeth Bowen. "You are never alone."

✂

The gap between the way we live here and at home is a natural topic for curiosity, and, as the taboo most artists and academic people have against talking about money wears off—quite swiftly, as it happens—also for conversation.

How much did the renovations carried out between May 1986 and April 1987 cost? A handsome book in each of our bedrooms provides a brief narrative of the renovation and ravishing photographs of the results. Speculation ranges from six to twenty million dollars, but the correct figure, it turns out, is a little over four million dollars.

How much does it cost the Foundation to host one resident and spouse for a month? Again estimates run high—there's wishful thinking among us. The tab is about six thousand dollars. Let's see, somebody says, there are 165 residents a year. . . .

How big is the staff? What is the entire annual budget for the Rockefeller Foundation? Sixty-five million dollars. At let's say, 9 percent, since surely the Rockefeller Foundation knows where to find better interest rates than people with passbook savings accounts, what is the total sum of which sixty-five million dollars would be the interest? How much does a silk scarf like that one cost at *Centro della Seta* in Como? How many lire to the dollar today?

✂

What our culture calls art may well have its prehistoric origins in the need to eroticize work. Survival was drudgery, but crucial drudgery, and flourish stayed eyes from glazing and attention from wandering. To scratch at the earth for edible roots was one thing, and to scratch at the earth for edible roots while thinking of sexual energy was another.

Freud argues rather elegantly in one of his *Introductory Lectures to Psychoanalysis* that an original need to eroticize work accounts for the durability of dream symbols and why they're drenched in sexuality. Each generation, framing the problem anew in its own era, recapitulates the original solution.

Maybe so. In any case, a diversion that first enlivened work grew to be one of the goals of work. Eventually humans scratched at the earth to build Kew Gardens.

Suppose that the object of work, in addition to whatever specific need it addresses, is to be done with it, to reach what we moderns call leisure. And suppose further that leisure is not a commodity (time is not, after all, money), an end in itself, but the oxygen of art.

✺

"It was a Sunday afternoon, wet and cheerless: and a duller spectacle this earth of ours has not to show than a rainy Sunday afternoon in London," wrote De Quincey.

Of course at the Villa it doesn't matter a whit what day of the week it is, but we're all, we residents, living by clocks set in our ordinary lives, and so on Sunday morning we dawdle a little at the breakfast table and look bereft for not having a fat newspaper to plod through.

A bee the size of a Ping-Pong ball tends the snapdragons below my studio window.

We residents belonged to a privileged class even before we came here. We don't have to get through work, and then through the fatigue caused by work, and then through the restless luxury of having no work to do, all in order to arrive at that leisure in which art gets matter-of-factly made.

To those who do the real material work of the world— farming, shoemaking, cooking—the Genesis story is about powerfully familiar rhythms, six days on and one off. To writers, who on Sunday afternoons stare indolently out their studio windows and then work dreamily, happily and hard, the story may well be, in part, a narcissistic fantasy in which the grateful creation, at the end of the performance, rises up to cry out, "Author, Author."

✸

At lunch R.C. reports that San Francisco is suffering an infestation of ants. It's because of the drought; they're looking for water. Sometimes they sojourn in the plumbing and come into the kitchen or bathroom from the faucet.

Of course we're a long way from home and might well receive this news the way winter vacationers in Florida read about blizzards where they live.

But how far from home are we? Why are we having a little trouble sleeping; why do we dream luridly when we do? The link to home may be stretched taut, but it therefore binds us all the more firmly.

There are about twenty of us around the table. One glass is full of *acqua minerale* and the other of Pinot Bianco. There's melon in port, an elegant little rice salad, halved tomatoes stuffed with Russian salad. Out the dining room windows the mountains are a shadowy wash, as in a watercolor, of gray and green against a blurred sky. There's a kind of rash or prickle in the air, just outside the circumference of any of our abilities to mention it, until later, of course, which is when I'm writing this.

Between breakfast and lunch five of our company have left, their time here elapsed. The farewells were a bloodbath of sentimentality, quite heartfelt for that matter, but drawn out in a way that ceremonies can be when they don't find a way to express their urgencies directly. If these departures had been a wedding, they'd make an overwhelming advertisement for elopement.

By 3:30 or so the sky will begin to darken, and in fifteen minutes more the heat-fueled cicadas will shut down. The wind that wasn't here at lunch will swirl and then lapse. Heat lightning will ramify across the sky. A first few fat raindrops will splat against the oak leaves outside my studio window, and then the wind will accelerate and the rain come hard, turning to hail that pings against the windows I'll have just shut.

But for now none of this has happened yet. The waiters are bringing coffee. My tennis date with M. is set for 5:00. Our departed colleagues are headed home. "Isn't this wonderful?" one of us mumbles to no one in particular.

✄

"If you cry on your birthday, you'll cry the year round," somebody's grandmother warned, maybe mine. Mine did tell me, "Bill, don't ever grow old," daring me to find a way to follow her advice.

Maybe I've tried. "I hate long farewells," I always say, and I've learned a way of leaving parties that's more like evaporation than any means of travel. I tend to "forget" birthdays and anniversaries, which is to say I remember them all too well and then let them slip by the way I leave parties. I try to cover these lapses with a brusque disregard for sentiment, but the fact is that every escaped ceremony is gone for good and that not marking them is like putting a headstone on each one.

Did I start this passage with a jaunty tone? It's already got a limp.

✄

Grief, as Samuel Johnson, that great procrastinator, once snapped at Mrs. Thrale, is a species of procrastination.

✄

This morning when I arrive at the post office there's a hand-lettered sign on the clerk's window:

NO STAMPS
THEY ARE FINISH

Nevertheless there's a small line, and this is, after all, Italy, so I stay in line to see what's what. By now the clerk knows me, so when I get to the head of the line and flourish a small handful of letters already stickered *Per Via Aerea*, she knows what I want. She weighs the letters and sells me the stamps. I step aside to lick them and an elderly Italian woman dressed in threadbare black replaces me. Her letters are for destinations inside Italy. The clerk reminds her in Italian of the sign in English and sends her away. The old woman looks at me licking my stamps.

"*Buon giorno,*" I say.

"*Buon giorno,*" she replies.

❧

The forging of alliances with peers and potential rivals by means of negotiated marriages was a standard feature among the families (the Sforzas, Malatestas, Montefeltros) who fiercely controlled the powerful northern Italian city states during the Renaissance, and the Gonzagas of Mantua held up their end despite the high percentage of hunchbacks born into the family line. This is the sort of moral cheerleading that might comfort Franco on a lonely, cloud-thronged night, but not for long, and besides, I don't want an opera whose arias are full of information. What Franco seethes for is that pure current of feeling that opera seems invented to convey, which makes opera so easily the butt of cruel jokes about its rickety artifices, its love of splendor and stage business for their own sakes, and how long it takes a stabbed person to die on stage. After all, little of life is about pure feeling; our daily bread is baked with mixed feelings and eaten with ambivalence. Pure feeling requires elaboration to stage and distance to enjoy.

In the final scene of act 1 of *Tredice Gobbi,* Franco is alone at center stage. The patchwork tile-roofed skyline of the sleeping town is behind him in dark silhouette. Is the silence of his loved one, far away in another town, a stark token of her faithlessness and disdain? A projection of his fears that he is worthless and misshapen and unlovable? Each day the mails bring him nothing. As the night sky clears and a burnished moon, like a heraldic wafer, rises above the roofs of his hometown, Franco wrings from his turbid heart his famous aria, *O posta inutile.*

❧

The Villa is a "Study and Conference Center." We residents study, or write or paint or compose. Now and then whole groups arrive for a conference. During one, there's a seating chart for dinner, so that members of the conference and residents are thrown into conversation.

Participants in the migration conference are mostly middle-aged white men who speak among themselves of past and future conferences, as if the migration in which they are expert were their own. The current conference on "development" in Africa and Southeast Asia is another matter. One night I am seated next to a gregarious and quick-witted Senegalese man of vast learning and the doomed gaiety that skillful, privileged Africans have developed to bridge the growing gap between their individual fates and the slow fates of their homelands. Another night I sit next to a Thai expert on the "informal sector" of the economy. "What's that?" I ask. "Black market, white market, everything unregulated." Once he discovers I am a poet it is easy for him to describe his interest in economics. "It's like Yeats. Gyres, Hindu stuff. Not the linear stuff the Marxists love."

Tonight, a soignée Tanzanian woman who leads expeditions of theater people into rural areas to try to provoke community theater there. "Of course, that's not what everyone means by development," she says, smiling dazzlingly.

The migration mavens look at us as if we are expensive, sulky children—us? guests of the Rockefeller Foundation too?—and they are busy fathers.

But the Africans and Asians are cheerful and like to mingle.

Among the Africans a standard joke takes place in the reading room. One has a newspaper in his hand and says casually, "I see there's been a *coup d'état* in your country."

The Asians play things closer to the chest, but they talk of jailings and confiscated research notes.

My Chinese friend, a river and delta expert, and his wife were rusticated for six years during the Cultural Revolution. The Red Guard left their daughter at home. The other villagers were too terrified to take her in, he allows, but they looked after her. I make a bitter little joke about measured charity, but I can't tell how it crosses the language barrier, since I have no Chinese. I'll never know. My friend laughs an odd sort of one-note sound, like a dog that has started to bark and thought violently better of it.

When the conferees have gone, my Chinese friend and I and all the other residents, with our anecdotes about the leisure of the theory class, will stay briefly behind; soon we'll be back in our several worlds, some of them cheerfully uninterested in our work, for the most part, and some savagely concerned.

✕

Tonight dinner will be a picnic near the Conference Center. It will be cool and relaxing to stare out across the Lecco branch of the lake and not to wear, in this heat, the coat and tie I customarily don for dinner.

Some residents balk at the formalities we observe. One of the men will sidle over to the waiter serving drinks before dinner and, running a finger between his collar and neck, say that he'd just as soon dispense with the coat and tie when it gets *this* hot. The waiter, in uniform, nods. This is a kind of solidarity; it's likely the resident is more uncomfortable being waited on than staining his collar with sweat.

It's wonderful to have food this good served to us daily, and to have little to do but work. As Pliny the Younger put it,

> Why not, before it is too late, hand over to others the cares of life and in this shaded sanctuary devote yourself to intellectual pursuits?

Phrased that way, the question's only answer is "Why not?"

As for me, I find the formalities welcome after a day of silence and passion and drudgery at the desk.

But the formalities, along with the sheer size and expense of the property, its commanding position on the promontory, the smooth and barely visible efficiency with which the Center is run and the refined taste according to which it has recently been renovated—all these combine to remind us at what huge distance art conventionally operates from survival.

It's because we sense how much grinding peasant life has been endured near marble quarries that the Villa raises mixed feelings in us, and it should: that's one of the functions of art.

If it hasn't been marinated in misery and if it can't convey that to us, then it's no longer art.

The cost of renovating the Villa Serbelloni or the prices fetched for paintings in the auction houses are useful footnotes to the histories of taste and economics, but what makes art valuable is the gravid pull of emotional life against which any artisan or artist struggles to keep a work of art from being pulled routinely down, like the makers of art themselves, into the receptive earth.

That's why making art is so hard. Of course it's playful and sensuous and exhilarating. But the raw material, the basic value, the human emotion of a moment, is not designed to endure, but to decay.

✖

The reason we residents at the Villa Serbelloni were so obsessed by the gap between the way we lived there and the way we lived at home was that we'd been temporarily promoted several rungs on the class ladder and had unsettingly mixed feelings about it. This unusual circumstance was, but for the unbroken time to work and the people I met there, the most valuable part of the experience for me.

The fiction most artists operate by is that we stand, somehow, outside the American class structure. Romantically anachronistic comparisons of poets to troubadours (or scholars to monks, for that matter) represent a wish to be outside, or at the farthest margins of, the economic structure. The truth is that, like the students many of us teach for a living, we belong to a subsidized bohemian class.

One function of a class is to provide its members with a negotiable map of experience rich enough to stand, as the part for the whole, for all experience. It has its rituals (graduate school as boot camp, tenure as officers' candidacy) and its costumes (if this class didn't exist, would a single corduroy sports coat ever be sold?), its dialects ("as it were"), and so on. There's enough of a culture in a class so that the incurious need never travel, and indeed, most Americans die in the class they were born in, for we have, despite our great consoling myths on the subject, almost no class mobility.

A month at Bellagio threw us all, quite as artificially as an opera works, into the dotty atavistic European world of "stately homes," as the British euphemism has it, and among tattered members of the nobility with private collections of important paintings. It's what's left of court life. The Rockefeller Foundation has inherited the benign prerogatives of the Sforzas.

One day a group of the residents, upon hearing that Princeton University might put its villa near Bellagio on the market, took a ferry across the lake to have a look at it, the way a dreamily ambitious young couple might take a Sunday afternoon drive through the nicest part of town.

And why not? Soon enough we'd all be home again, and that young couple, too.

✳

The walls and stone steps and gravel paths between the main building at the Villa and the Marenese, where I have my room and studio, are rife with lizards. When they hear footsteps, they sometimes freeze. More or less stone colored, they're then hard to see until you learn how to look for them. But more often they launch themselves on mad scrambles out of your way, slithering into crevices, diving into the bases of bushes, hurling themselves over the lips of one of the terraced garden's many levels. If you stop to peer over after them— some of the levels are twelve feet below the one above—you find them clinging to sprigs and outcroppings just over the lip, panting and stiffened to blend in with their lizard-colored world.

They range from those that are maybe eight inches long to one panicked *bambino* tinier than my little finger who hadn't memorized the escape drill and scrawled along the path in front of me, passing crevice after crevice and lip after lip, never simply veering off to one side or the other. I stopped, then, to give him a break, and he huffed mightily up at me from the pathway, calmed himself down, and then idled more slowly than you please from the middle of the path to the edge. It must have taken five whole stately seconds. Well, I thought, as I paused for a couple beats and then walked on to breakfast, there's two of us hugely pleased with ourselves already, and it's early.

One of the values of metaphor is to store the whole panoply of remembered sensual life as compactly as possible in case we have to travel light, and I think we do. I'll be able to carry the whole weight of my stay in the image of any one of these variously patterned and colored lizards, and I've got my candidate in mind.

Swiftly the heat will be vivid again, and the dull nag in my calves from climbing steps, the lithe cypresses soaring up from the gardens, the water blue-gray under its scrim of mist and haze. . . . And, darting out and scribbling furiously across the gravel pathway, like a full emotion rescued from the sentimental and sloppy filing system of memory, a tiny lizard, the whole of it beating like a heart with legs.

※

Act 3 of *Tredice Gobbi* begins with the celebrated aria in which Dottore Claro, Franco's psychoanalyst, explains to him that La Diretta is a "transitional object," a viaduct from his raging infantile needs to an appropriate and adult love rich in mixed feelings, such as he bears for his sweetie in a faraway town. What is her name *(Como se dice?)*, Dottore Claro teasingly wonders.

Franco is eager to reply but their time is up. *Più tarde,* he sings mournfully. Geese snooze on the municipal pond. A dozen rueful hunchbacks sing curfew. Across the proscenium slithers the shadow of the Lizard King. His loved one is far, far away.

※

Usually poetry is written in brief, fierce bursts; three or four hours at the highest concentration is a good day's work, as it would be for an athlete or dancer. So a residency like this one, in which time lies richly ahead like a fertile valley or a month of Sundays, is a challenge to a poet's ingenuity.

But wait! One could contrive a kind of fictional journal, a series of apparently random meditations and observations on what it feels like to be here. The duff and litter and scrap that poetry fails to burn away would be the favored material to work with, the way a magpie builds a nest.

When the word *accident* first came into English, it had only a very specific theological meaning. "Substance" meant that part (the majority) of the bread and wine that was transubstantiated into the body and blood of Christ; the "accidents" were the crumbs and droplets left over. In Italian, *accidente* is an imprecation against bad luck.

The piece would lavish all its love on the accidental. And of course work on it would fill the glass of one's days.

When I was a small boy I spent late Sunday afternoons listening to radio thrillers. There were three hours of them: "Sky King," "Nick Carter, Private Detective," "The Shadow," "The Lone Ranger," "The Green Hornet," and for the sixth half-hour a silly show about a bunch of kids who lived with perfect parents on a ranch where there was no apparent work or livestock—what the kids did with their time was solve mysteries. But by the time this program came on I listened to it, too, for the trance was on me.

The spell was most powerful in winter, for then the three hours began in fading light and ended in darkness. I went to my room and closed the door and by the time the evening adult programs came on the air it would be dark inside and out, no light but the yellow-orange glow, like the imagination's pilot light, on the radio dial.

Later some of the programs were transplanted to television, but I hated them. Radio allowed me to imagine voluptuously and continually; television gave me its images and mine were routed. "The Lone Ranger" was especially paltry. No matter what the script conjured, the actors kept riding up to and around the same drab boulder.

Reading replaced television for me soon enough, but that rock is still with me. These days it stands for the dead weight of joylessness. It seems to have been built by a series of minute secretions: inattentions, work not done, evaded pleasures, dull and compulsive responses to a rich world. The Lone Ranger who rides up to it at intervals is a haggard and grandiose version of me. The mask fools no one. He seems to belong to the rock the way a ghost belongs to a house, to be trying to haunt his own depression.

Of course on the back lot of Universal Studios the rock was probably built of papier-mâché, and thus ridiculously easy to lift and no dead weight at all. Here comes the Lone Ranger riding up to it again. I watch him closely. He dismounts. He makes the thumbs-up sign and winks.

✄

Maybe that's what I felt like when I got here. In a month emotional life, like a river, cuts many a meander, and can't tell you exactly where its been, though there are hints in the debris it sweeps along downstream. I had thought I'd be leaving daily life behind in order to work, in Donald Justice's lovely phrase, at "that distance from life we conventionally call art," but where was my daily life but here?

I'd wandered the property to find the Merlot vines from which the wine with the Villa Serbelloni label we'd been served was made and popped an immature grape (July) into my mouth. I'd swum in the scouringly cold lake water. I'd wakened at four in the morning to throw my bedroom window open and watch an electrical storm roll down from the Alps and use the whole skyscape above the lakes to play itself out.

On the property I'd found three caches of idle reading, summer or airplane reading, call it what you will. A Simenon, a Robert Ludlum, *Gone with the Wind,* a couple of gothics with brooding houses and handsome heroes (or is it handsome houses and brooding heroes?) on the cover. A James Bond novel, not by Ian Fleming but by the man who after Fleming's death was appointed to keep the profits from the Bond series cryonically aflicker. The transcripts of the White House tapes. All paperbacks. You take them away like Cokes and bring back the empties, except that they're still full, being books; though, being the books they are, they're only more or less full.

Reading a few thrillers I extracted from this selection was daily life, and so was an afternoon I found and devoured

Edna O'Brien's *A Pagan Place:* the real thing, with all its emotional risk and erotic thrall and bravery, the kind of book that turns people into readers and writers in the first place.

Is not daily life our great good and glory, though we sometimes speak of it as a tedium? Perhaps I should replace that "though" with "and." Here Ella Walker, whiskey heiress, became Her Serene Highness, Principessa della Torre e Tasso. With that title came the right never to be spoken to unless she initiated the conversation, though I have no way of knowing if she relished the right or not. I have been told that when she walked on her property, her staff and gardeners, assuming that she'd be pleased, hid themselves behind the trees and topiary so she could have the illusion of being alone. It is a complicated life in which the most radical fact of being human, one's own essential solitude, is staged and choreographed by a staff of seventy, but Ella Walker makes, as we imagine her surveying the serenity of her gardens, a wonderful figure for the fierce ambivalence with which we seek and deny the tang of our own loneliness.

❌

Most people leave in the morning, and we've heard that while you're at breakfast, somebody takes the nametag off your door, so that when you go back to herd your baggage to the taxi, your room is already anonymous. And we've heard that after you leave, your room is fumigated before its next inhabitants come in.

But from whom have we heard these folktales? From each other. There is no truth to them, except that they reflect an anxiety some of us feel about going back to that other daily life from which we've been so wonderfully and, with diligence and luck, productively on vacation.

"I wonder what lunch will be?" one departing resident mumbled at breakfast.

"Pasta," I said, "tiny effigies of the departed."

❌

The silent menace with which the black gondola glides across the stage in act 3 of *La Gioconda* is the model for the departure scene I imagine as the culmination of *Tredice Gobbi*. A black taxi scrunches across the gravel driveway of the Villa. A swarm of hunchbacks in porters' uniforms contest for Franco's luggage. Thunder rumbles and geese dither.

But Franco isn't going anywhere; he's a fictional character. In Verona you can see Juliet's balcony and tomb, and Romeo's house, but you might as well go to some small village in Greece to see Homer's mother's microwave oven. If a nonfictional Juliet had existed, her balcony, if she had one, might have looked like this one—it's the right period and visitors will want to see it in any case.

It's I who steps into the taxi.

What would the lake look like on a gray day in late October, the soft air above it streaked by chill rain? What will become of the tobacconist's crippled daughter? One day when neither of them knew I was watching I saw him patiently tease her from a lumpish glower into a spray of laughter. How soon will the Merlot grapes be ready to crush? What mail will be piled up for me when I get home?

"So long," I cry, and down the driveway swirls the taxi. Time to go home. I've got work to do.

(1989)

Dull Subjects

"And what are your poems about?" a poet might be asked by, let's say, an affable seatmate on an airplane. And what would our poet say?

The question makes immediate sense about other sorts of books, and answers are not hard to imagine.

"*Unsafe at Any Speed* is about the wanton and cynical triumph of style over safety in American-built automobiles," said Mr. Nader.

"It's an odd book," said Mr. Melville, ringing the stewardess's bell with, among the other objects in his teeming mind, a second Bloody Mary in view. "A one-legged whaling captain monomaniacally pursues a white whale. It's a novel about whaling, male bonding, obsession, and it's about the mute and lulling allure that ideas of good and evil bear for Americans. It's hard to talk about; that's why I wrote the book." Mr. Melville heaved an ambiguous noise, a sort of stifled, ecstatic sigh, and for that instant it was hard to know if he was satisfied by his *précis* or only beginning to describe.

"*New Hope for the Dead* is the ultimate self-help book," its author explained.

Robert Creeley has used as an essay title a puzzled question once asked him: "Are those real poems or did you make them up yourself?"

Among the other confusions behind the question posed to Creeley is a predisposition to the idea that all real poems were written by people now dead, and since Creeley is alive he must be an imposter. Also important here is the notion that poetry should not be merely personal, that someone inspired, as a poet in the popular imagination must be, has breathed in the spirit of poetry and is temporarily the vessel and conduit of some larger force, as indeed we all are until we cease to inhale.

But, paradoxically, poetry in the popular imagination is assumed to be among the most personal of the arts, if not the most personal of them, and indeed, doesn't the durable injunction against the merely personal suggest how prevalent the merely personal might be?

Perhaps we could begin thinking about the use of subject matter to poetry by considering the poet's needs. Here is a brief excerpt from an interview with James Merrill.

> You hardly ever need to *state* your feelings. The point is to feel and keep the eyes open. Then what you feel is expressed, is mimed back at you by the scene. A room, a landscape. I'd go a step further. *We* don't *know* what we feel until we see it distanced by this kind of translation.

Merrill is close here to drawing the body of Eliot's elusive Cheshire Cat, the "objective correlative." It isn't that you know what you feel and devise alchemically a scrap of language that transmits accurately such complex information to a reader. The implicit model for such a process, were it possible, is the genetic code. With that thought in mind we can see how much hubris has been attached by others to Eliot's modest catch phrase.

The poet is struggling to make something, and then, secondarily if it comes to that, to make something clear. Something subjective, of which one was the helpless owner, is ex-pressed, pushed out, made objective. Both poet and reader can now gaze on it with some curiosity, for it is in this world a new thing. It is, so far as words can create such effects, palpable, malleable, mysterious, in all three of these ways like matter itself. That the poet and reader, or any two observers, might describe it quite differently goes, almost, without saying.

A poet beginning to make something needs raw material, something to transform. An ambition or a hope to transform suggests a process, and so a good analogy for subject matter in poetry might be a chunk of matter with process already alive in it, like mother of vinegar or sourdough starter. Or like decay.

If subject matter is chosen in order that it be transformed, then a Subject Index to Poetry would be an especially unneeded and impossible reference work.

Indeed it must seem to those as casually curious about poetry as Creeley's interlocutor that poetry has all too few subjects, and I suspect the earnest compilers of a Subject Index to Poetry would find their major headings both borderless and few. To forestall such fruitless labors, I hereby offer a short but comprehensive summary of subjects for lyric poetry.

1. I went out into the woods today and it made me feel, you know, sort of religious.
2. We're not getting any younger.
3. It sure is cold and lonely (a) without you, honey, or (b) with you, honey.
4. Sadness seems but the other side of the coin of happiness, and vice versa, and in any case the coin is too soon spent and on we know not what.

One could, I suppose, if one were possessed of a mania for condensation and categorization, offer a single ur-plot for lyric poetry and indeed for all imaginative literature, and if so, one could do worse than the following four-word sentence, a plot summary of the Bob Hope, Bing Crosby and Dorothy Lamour film, *The Road to Bali*: "Amorous gorilla pursues Hope."

Hope is the most difficult of industries, for it manufactures nothing from something. But poems make something out of only a little more than nothing. It is perhaps in fear of the generative power of the best poetry that so much bad discussion of poetry reduces the fully exfoliated poem to a seed, the poem's theme or topic, which of course is not what the poem grew from but a poor, bare paraphrase of what the poem grew to be if every leaf and bud and detail be ignored and an idea be made to stand for the poem the way in children's drawings a stick figure is made to stand for a person.

Our Subject Index to Poetry, then, would turn out to be a Theme Index to Poetry—even less useful than we first supposed.

Let's consider the way so many passages by Wallace Stevens turn on a quick shift of perspective.

> In my room, the world is beyond my understanding;
> But when I walk I see that it consists of three or four hills
>   and a cloud.

So begins "Of the Surface of Things," and here is the third of "Six Significant Landscapes."

> I measure myself
> Against a tall tree.
> I find that I am much taller,
> For I reach right up to the sun,
> With my eye;
> And I reach to the shore of the sea
> With my ear.
> Nevertheless, I dislike
> The way the ants crawl
> In and out of my shadow.

And here is the eleventh of "Thirteen Ways of Looking at a Blackbird."

> He rode over Connecticut
> In a glass coach.
> Once, a fear pierced him,
> In that he mistook
> The shadow of his equipage
> For blackbirds.

There is always in poetry a kind of plot. After all, grammar has a plot: sentences open and then, according to the rules and habits of grammar and syntax, they close. And in a poem line 1 precedes line 2. So the two primary units of a poem, the grammatical unit and the line, both have built into them considerations of time and rhythm, which is to say narrative and suspense.

In poems where large and readily recognizable events are the controlling elements of plot and narrative—let's take obvious examples like "Casey at the Bat" or "Gunga Din" or "The Highwayman"—subject matter may well be the single controlling factor in a reader's response. There are plenty of baseball fans who know "Casey at the Bat" who don't know Marianne Moore's various passages of encomium to the Brooklyn Dodgers. The difference in appeal to such a reader between Ernest Thayer's ballad and Marianne Moore's lines is likely to be that for Moore, subject matter is not in itself important, except that it gives her the opportunity to speak about something that engages her passions. What is important instead is what she can discover to say.

In passages like those I've quoted from Stevens, where the ordinary elements of drama, conflict and narrative suspense are almost wholly suppressed, we have a clear opportunity to see how provisional ostensible subject matter is.

In a poem where subject matter is the finish line for discovery, rather than the start, a first line like

In my room, the world is beyond my understanding.

would lead, probably, to a quest: the speaker would go into the larger world, undergo significant experiences, and, likely as not, return symmetrically to his room, older but wiser.

But the speaker in Stevens's poem goes out and finds, without insisting that the event increases his understanding, that when he is outside the world consists of what he can see of it.

In the passage from "Six Significant Landscapes" we could almost be hearing the preternaturally intelligent babble of an immense, precocious baby. The discovery that the senses are an extension of the body, in lines 3–7, recapitulates a recognizable stage in infant development, and there is in the switch between this discovery and the imperious dislike of the ants (what are *they* doing to *my* world, which is my body) a very small child's promiscuous attention to the world as a waterfall of sensations.

About the passage from "Thirteen Ways of Looking at a Blackbird" we should note how thoroughly unanswered are questions the passage might provoke in a reader for whom subject matter is a resting place.

Where do you get a glass coach outside of fairy tales? Why Connecticut? Were blackbirds in themselves fearful? or the mistake of the shadow of one thing, a glass coach, for many blackbirds? Or what?

Stevens has a short poem in *Harmonium* called "Theory" that seems apposite.

> I am what is around me.
>
> Women understand this.
> One is not duchess
> A hundred yards from a carriage.
>
> These, then, are portraits:
> A black vestibule;
> A high bed sheltered by curtains.
>
> These are merely instances.

The first sentence is a tautology, we could say, the way all sentences using the verb *to be* tend toward being tautologies. I don't mean to suggest by the word "tautology" that the sentence is self-evident. For one thing, Stevens's proposition about the nature of the self is not an ordinarily creditable one. And for another, the whole notion of self-evidence is a problem, for what we call "self-evident" is only so after we have noticed it; before that moment it was invisible. What I mean to emphasize is the way the verb *to be* resembles, in mathematical notation, an equals sign. It's like a fulcrum, and it balances the two halves of the sentence by the variable poise of a teeter-totter.

So if a person can be what is around that person, a temporary portrait or an instance of that person can be made by sketching a scene or situation. As if to underscore how one can serve for the other. Stevens gives us two instances where the person would in fact be hard to see, hidden by the scene that is, anyway, that person. So what does it matter that this person's face is hard or impossible to see in a black vestibule? It probably doesn't matter, even, if the person in question is inside the sheltering curtains of a high bed when we look at the bed or is out, somewhere else, touring Connecticut in a glass equipage, let's say, and merely might as well be behind those sheltering curtains.

But these portraits aren't emblems, they're instances: they're in rather than out of time, and that's why, I take it, fastidious Stevens adds the word "merely."

Subject matter, then, is often in poetry a place to begin, and it need not, we can see from an admiring glance at these few passages from Stevens, refer to an event or to a drama larger or more melodramatic than the shifting play of perception.

Sometimes poems refer for their beginnings to exactly those topics conventional wisdom considers so dull that even knaves know it: weather, how time flies, how grass grows, etc. William Carlos Williams's celebrated "Spring and All" touches on all these dull subjects and more.

> By the road to the contagious hospital
> under the surge of the blue
> mottled clouds driven from the
> northeast—a cold wind. Beyond, the
> waste of broad, muddy fields
> brown with dried weeds, standing and fallen
>
> patches of standing water
> the scattering of tall trees
>
> All along the road the reddish
> purplish, forked, upstanding, twiggy
> stuff of bushes and small trees
> with dead, brown leaves under them
> leafless vines—
>
> Lifeless in appearance, sluggish
> dazed spring approaches—

They enter the new world naked,
cold, uncertain of all
save that they enter. All about them
the cold, familiar wind—

Now the grass, tomorrow
the stiff curl of wildcarrot leaf
One by one objects are defined—
It quickens: clarity, outline of leaf

But now the stark dignity of
entrance—Still, the profound change
has come upon them: rooted, they
grip down and begin to awaken.

Reading this poem again during a summer of Bread and Circuses—two political conventions, the grandiloquent tedium of the endless presidential campaign. ABC's jingoistic Gee Whiz coverage of the Olympics—is a great, grounding pleasure.

Often in poems incomplete sentences mean incomplete thoughts and emotions, but in this poem, where we don't have a technically complete sentence until the fourth stanza, what seems missing at first is exactly what a verb is for—process, change. They go on overhead, in weather, but the ground on which Williams's eye is fixed is strewn with stuff: matter seen at a stage almost before growth has given it form. It barely has color (not red, but reddish; not purple, but purplish). It's in waste, without apparent pattern or meaning. It's sluggish and dazed and uncertain.

I can't think just now of a poem that celebrates better the usual work of the vegetable world, nor of a poem that makes more gracefully the analogy of such work to the endless and ordinary labor of human consciousness. After a summer of tatty glory and hypnotized praise of a selective American past, it's good to dowse one's dusty face in the stream of Williams's poem, made, like life itself, from scruff and blur and effort, into, at life's best, clarity and outline and shadowing.

"What is there here but weather?" Stevens asks in "Waving Adieu, Adieu, Adieu," a poem aching from the speed by which one perception is replaced by the next.

That would be waving and that would be crying,
Crying and shouting and meaning farewell,
Farewell in the eyes and farewell at the centre,
Just to stand still without moving a hand.

In a world without heaven to follow, the stops
Would be endings, more poignant than partings,
    profounder,
And that would be saying farewell, repeating farewell,
Just to be there and just to behold.

To be one's singular self, to despise
The being that yielded so little, acquired
So little, too little to care, to turn
To the ever-jubilant weather, to sip

One's cup and never to say a word,
Or to sleep or just to lie there still,
Just to be there, just to be beheld,
That would be bidding farewell, be bidding farewell.

One likes to practice the thing. They practice,
Enough, for heaven. Ever-jubilant,
What is there here but weather, what spirit
Have I except it comes from the sun?

It's not only that dull—or modest, or unassuming—
subjects provide a useful place to begin, or that they can be
in themselves a constraint against melodrama and easy gran-
deur. Inherently dramatic and shapely subject matter lends
itself to a certain neatness—conflict, resolution, and calm—
that may appeal to a poet's craft and perfectionism, on the
one hand, but may well, on the other hand, incite a poet's
suspicion of the perfected certainties of art in the face of a
life—not the poet's, necessarily, but anyone's—that is unruly,
unfinished, and unstoppable.

Here is Howard Moss's "The Summer Thunder."

Now the equivocal lightning flashes
Come too close for comfort and the thunder
Sends the trembling dog under the table,
I long for the voice that is never shaken.

Above the sideboard, representation
Takes its last stand: a small rectangle
Of oak trees dripping with a painted greenness,
And in the foreground, a girl asleep

In a field who speaks for a different summer
From the one the thunder is mulling over—
How calm the sensuous is! How saintly!
Undersea light from a lit-up glen

Lends perspective to an arranged enchantment,
As peaceful as a Renaissance courtyard
Opened for tourists centuries after
Knights have bloodied themselves with doctrine.

The first stanza bristles with a nearly subliminal syntactical
discontent like that caused by shifting barometric pressure
before rain. At the end of each of the first two lines, the
grammar of the unfolding sentence is in doubt: (1) Is *flashes* a
verb or a noun? (2) Is *thunder* part of a dual noun—*comfort and
the thunder*—or is it the beginning of a new clause beginning
with "and"?

And consider the understanding that makes possible the
link between "perspective" and "arranged enchantment" and
"doctrine"; this short lyric poem contains not a theory but an
understanding of the relationship between technique in paint-
ing and technique in religion. No wonder "sensuous" and
"saintly," at first glance an odd pair of adjectives, snuggle
comfortably together in line 11, bonded by an idea of contain-
ment, contentment even, that we are lured to by its promise of
respite from thunder at the poem's beginning—and eager to
escape from, as from blood, by the poem's end.

The ability to hold such opposites in balance without resort
to mere paradox is a signature of our best writing. A related
passage is in Vladimir Nabokov's *Speak Memory.*

Nabokov's beloved father is, after memory itself, the hero of
his memoir. His father is being tossed from a blanket by villag-
ers who are ceremonially celebrating his father's role in settling
a local dispute. The custom is like the one in which the cox-
swain of a winning crew is thrown into the water after a race. I

mention this only to point out that it has nothing to do with the intellectually lazy and politically sentimental view of Nabokov's family as White Russians, those stuffed reactionaries coddling Fabergé eggs in the Wax Museum of Political Stereotypes. Nabokov's father was in fact a leader of the Kadets (a liberal opposition party before the Revolution), was jailed for issuing a revolutionary manifesto, and died in 1922 in Berlin, at an emigré political meeting, when he stepped in front of a speaker who was the target of two monarchist assassins.

> From my place at table I would suddenly see through one of the west windows a marvelous case of levitation. There, for an instant, the figure of my father in his wind-rippled white summer suit would be displayed, gloriously sprawling in midair, his limbs in a curiously casual attitude, his handsome, imperturbable features turned to the sky. Thrice, to the mighty heave-ho of his invisible tossers, he would fly up in this fashion, and the second time he would go higher than the first and then there he would be, on his last and loftiest flight, reclining, as if for good, against the cobalt blue of the summer noon, like one of those paradisiac personages who comfortably soar, with such a wealth of folds in their garments, on the vaulted ceiling of a church while below, one by one, the wax tapers in mortal hands light up to make a swarm of minute flames in the mist of incense, and the priest chants of eternal repose, and funeral lilies conceal the face of whoever lies there, among the swimming lights, in the open coffin.

Nabokov's famous phrase-making abilities are on full display in this virtuoso passage, but it is perhaps the stark and off-hand "as if for good" that is the most haunting in this hallucinatory performance. The more lovingly remembered and painstakingly rendered a loss is, the more on the one hand it is ours, and the more on the other hand it is already given over to memory and to art, which have, each of them, their own uses for loss. The clear light of Nabokov's prose shines on everything here, lingeringly (the tapers light up "one by one"), though it can't, or perhaps won't, penetrate the funeral lilies to illuminate the handsome and now wholly imperturbable features of Nabokov's father.

How easy it would have been for a lesser artist than Nabokov to make this scene conventionally picturesque and sentimental; indeed, it may well have given him considerable private pleasure to have picked an incident with such inducements to gauzy writing and to have persisted, with the apparently perverse courage that marks the true artist, to find in the *trompe l'oeil* of his father ascending into heaven the gravity of his real interest in the scene.

Oddly enough it is the incident that seems, at the start, already artistically shaped and full of feeling that is most likely to finish dull, perhaps because it conceals by its first appeal how much work can be done with it.

It is not, of course, the subject that is or isn't dull, but the quality of attention we do or do not pay to it, and the strength of our will to transform. Dull subjects are those we have failed.

(1985)

Lines

Nulla dies sine linea

Isak Dinesen's *Out of Africa* begins with aristocratic understatement: "I had a farm in Africa." She means "farm" the way the rich refer to their summer homes as "cottages." She had a coffee plantation, hundreds of acres.

Once in Houston I went to dinner with Amos Tutuola, the Nigerian fabulist (*The Palm-Wine Drinkard, My Life in the Bush of Ghosts*), and some fellow faculty in the writing program. Tutuola wore an embroidered robe and flip-flops. The restaurant? It must have been picked for convenient location. It had brass rails, Boston ferns, etched glass, groovy clientele and over-priced drinks: it should have been called "Lawyers in Love."

"Fish," said Tutuola, "I want fish."

"Very good, sir," said the waiter, a senior at Rice. One order of snapper. Takes all kinds.

"You have different fish here than we have at home," Tutuola observed.

The air was sparse with conversation. "What would you be doing now, at dusk, if you were at home?" one of us tried.

"Oh," he chortled, "oh. I'd be working on my farm." By "farm" he meant, a little more conversation discovered, a garden large enough that one needed the help of one's children to keep it up.

The next question he answered we hadn't had wit enough to ask. "Yams."

We'd all thought we knew what he meant by "farm." But what farm? The King Ranch? Horace's Sabine Farm? Baseball has a farm system, and there's the farm down on which you can't keep those who've seen Paris. There's Pepperidge Farm and Cold Comfort Farm. What's an ant farm? Part of any meaning of "farm" is the whole web of other meanings besides the one the speaker has primarily in mind.

Maybe that's how best to think about the line in poetry.

Line comes from the Greek *linon* and the Latin *linea*. *Linum* is the genus of flax, and indeed *linea* is the feminine of the adjective *lineus*, meaning flaxen. Samuel Johnson's dictionary gives two meanings: one, from Locke, is one-tenth of an inch, and the second is lint or flax. "Linen" is the closest English word to these sources, which also survive in "linnet"—the bird feeds on flaxseed—"linoleum," a word coined by the inventor of linoleum in 1863, and "crinoline," first made with woof of hair (L. *crinis*) and warp of linen.

According to Skeat, it made its way into English through the Anglo-Saxon *line* (thread, cord), and via French, *ligne* (stroke, row, rank, verse).

It's from the regularity of weaving, one suspects, that the line becomes straight: lineage, lineaments, linotype (line o' type), align, et al.

There are still many usages combining fabric or clothing with various literal and metaphorical senses of thread and cord. There's the fishing line, and there's the line of goods that a salesman peddles. A line of sportswear, let's say, or lingerie (which is in the etymological line). But it's also the sales pitch itself. Clothing is a form of salesmanship.

But salesmen used to call a steady customer—a draper or hosier, maybe—a good line. That regular customer was someone you might brag you had on the line, though these days the line is a telephone line, made no longer of wire but, as the advertisements cheerfully announce, of fiber optics. We can't begin to think about fiber optics or any optics without drawing or imagining lines.

Then there's the clothesline, both the one on which bed- and table-linens dried and the one ballplayers invoked to describe a line drive. Current ballplayers call that a frozen rope.

There used to be a line in West Coast jazz slang that meant

a lick, riff, or break, but that usage is as dated as "hepcat." On the other hand, there's this passage from Alan Lomax's *Mr. Jelly Roll.*

> You was considered out of line if your coat and pants matched. Many a time they would kid me, "Boy, you must be from the country. Here you got trousers on the same as your coat?"

To be out of line means to lack protective coloration, or to have the wrong coloration.

To be in line, or on line, as we say in New York, is to belong. There are kick lines and chorus lines, unemployment lines, ticket lines, etc. In the British Army all regular infantry regiments except the First Guards and the Rifle Brigade are called line regiments. Of course the British call a line of schoolchildren led by a teacher a crocodile (proportion of head to body?), and call a police line-up an identification parade.

And there are two derivations given for "to toe the line" in the various reference books at my immediate disposal. One is from British naval usage and means to form a rank or line, and the other means to step up to a mark on the floor at an identification parade.

There are sidelines, foul lines, out-of-bounds lines, red and blue lines, etc. Games are about rules.

Thus we have a line of work, and walk the line if we want to keep our jobs. Here the usages begin to blur wonderfully and instructively. For the line has always been about work, but it's also been about seduction, sales and buying, rules and breaking rules, being a soldier or a suspected criminal.

A sideline comes from sports, right? But a sideline is a second job, hobby, or avocation. What about the pimp with a string of girls? These "girls" have their electronic sisters who do telephone sex: lisping Lolitas, dominatrixes. . . . In cabbies' slang a "line-load" used to be a passenger bound for the red light district.

Well, sex, salesmanship, clothing business, and games are all woven together, right? Isn't that, we hear someone saying a little loudly from the bar, the bottom line? That figure is from accounting, of course, but what about to put it on the line, probably from gambling, or to toe the line, or to go down the line?

To go down the line likely stems from hobo slang and means to walk the wrong way against the paycheck line: you've been fired. Given that so many hobo figures come from railroad life, to go down the line may well mean to ride the rails, or, by extension, to go down the rails as far as prison.

Isn't the shortest distance between two points a straight line? "Euclid alone has looked on beauty bare," the first line of an Edna St. Vincent Millay sonnet has it. These are imaginary lines, like latitudes, longitudes, and the equator (in sailors' slang, crossing the line means to go from one hemisphere to the other). We use lines to measure what's resistant to measurement, to speak about the unspeakable. Hard lines—they're related to the British "hard cheese," an insincere condolence—mean the short straw. Palmistry has its "line of life."

What does "on the line" mean? According to *Brewer's Dictionary of Phrase and Fable:*

> Said of a picture that, at the Royal Academy, is hung in a position that places its centre at the level of the spectator's eye.

How tall is this spectator?

Does the spectator's coat have a lining? More from Brewer:

> When the court tailor wished to obtain the patronage of Beau Brummel, he made him a present of a dress-coat lined with bank-notes. Brummel wrote a letter of thanks stating that he quite approved of the coat, and especially admired the lining.

Of course lines are military: the long gray line, the Maginot line, the Mason-Dixon line.

The British have a thin red line to match our long gray line. The old Ninety-third Highlanders were so described at the Battle of Balaclava (1854) by W. H. Russell. The phrase has come to mean, by extension, British infantrymen in action. One can hear the pride in "thin"; it was thin, but it held.

We call that kind of understanding reading between the lines.

Actors learn their lines or fake lines. Most reference books give a theatrical source for "good lines," but given the burbling stew that language is, it's probably either a mistake or a sad necessity of compiling reference books to settle on only one source. Ships have "good lines," or conversely, a stubby and inelegant one has the lines of a butter dish. In some dictions women and horses have good lines, especially if they're expensive, and the word refers both to looks and lineage.

To reduce a woman to lines is bad sexual politics but can be good art: think of those Matisse nudes in which eight lines suggest a woman not only sexy but lively and intelligent, and embodying even that resistance to description we often call "spiritual." The word "nude" may be crucial here. The depicted woman isn't wearing lingerie, with its false etymological suggestions of "lounge" and "linger." The French word for linen is *linge*. In English as well as French the word once meant both underwear and sheets, which allowed Phineas Fletcher to write raffishly in 1614: "Love is like linen; often changed, the sweeter."

Of course in poetry there's "linage," as there once was in journalism; it means payment by the line.

"I croon my tears at fifty cents per line," as James Wright wrote in 1959. At most journals, the pay hasn't risen since.

Everyone knows from Pope about monosyllables in verse:

And ten low words oft creep in one dull line.

But American poetry may be different, or the American ear. E.g.,

Back out of all this now too much for us . . .

Ten low words, I suppose, but line them up the right way. . . .

Maybe it's not the ducks that matter, but having them in a row. I can remember in my high school days striding thoughtfully around a pool table in what I hoped was a creditable imitation of a good pool player, then squinting as I crouched to sight a combination. My cronies and I were ordinary players, but we prided ourselves on being able to conceive shots we might not, on account of rustiness and insouciance, be able to pull off. I'd stare thoughtfully at the alignment and then announce "It'll go" or "It won't go." We thought we were talking about a particular pool shot, but of course we were talking about our impersonations of more skilled and confident people than we were, and about the whole arc of the long lives before us. We were just "shooting a line," as an earlier slang would have had it. It's a kind of behavior lazily described by some as "male bonding," but the only and weak glue, it sometimes seems to me, was a shared terror and a shared, unspoken compact never to say the word "terror." Instead we said "It'll go."

We weren't old enough to know that the glory of language is its slurs and border-crossings, and that whenever we spoke about one thing we were speaking about many. It was already time for us to begin to learn this, but we were young and language would come in its slow fruitful time to teach some of us a little of what we needed to know. As for the rest, "it won't go."

There are wonderful usages that stand a little to the side of the tendency I've tried to illuminate here, the tendency of all originally specific meanings to blur and join with associated meanings.

From the late seventeenth to the early nineteenth century a kind of mock-courtly tone was used to describe a dram of brandy: "a line of the old author."

The *linea alba* is the proper anatomical name for that pale sluice of hair that runs from the bottom of your navel to the top of your pubic hair.

But think about them; these lines, too, live off the existence and power of other lines.

Nulla dies sine linea is attributed to the Greek artist, Appellos, and obviously enough not by a Greek. It means "No day without a line," and something about its call to industry sounds very Roman. Anthony Trollope took it for a motto.

(1987)

Anita O'Day and I

In 1957 I stood next to Anita O'Day at a concession stand at the Newport Jazz Festival. She took a first sip of coffee from a paper cup and gave it a glum look. Due onstage in an hour, she rummaged through her purse for a cigarette. Good God, I thought, it's Anita O'Day, toes and ears and all.

She wore an expression I now recognize from the inside out. There's a cartoon in William Steig's "Fellow Creatures" series that shows a middle-aged man in a sports coat on the balls of his feet, grinning. The caption? "Professor Greeting New Students with Pleasantries." And there have been entire literary parties through which I have helplessly carried a look like that on my face like a cheerful shadow.

"Honey," she asked, "have you got a light?" I lit her rumpled cigarette. And then I didn't back away, I didn't say anything, I just stood there. I was fifteen. "You havin' a good time?" she asked.

It was a smoker's voice, rumbly at the circumference, and I was so hypnotized by the pleasure of the moment that I confessed. "Right now I am." She looked at me slant. She let some smoke loll out of her mouth and rise into her nostrils. Who was this kid and did she need to be alarmed? She looked up at me with a sudden grin and said, "You'll be all right."

After all, I'd had a light, and whatever it was, it was done. Whatever it was, I took it as a prediction, and as an obligation, too.

(1989)

Richard Hugo and Detective Fiction

Late in his life Richard Hugo wrote a hard-boiled detective novel, *Death and the Good Life*. It's perhaps not surprising that a poet for whom guilt was a central theme loved to read such books. Who reads detective fiction? Auden wrote, "I suspect that the typical reader of detective fiction is, like myself, a person who suffers from a sense of sin." The word "sin" is too theological for Hugo, but if we substitute "guilt" or "shame" the sentence is apposite.

Auden was thinking primarily of the British detective novel, whereas Hugo loved the American version whose major practitioners are Dashiel Hammett, Raymond Chandler and Ross Macdonald. The detectives in such books are hard-nosed and soft-hearted, loners suspended between the criminal world and the world of official justice, people for whom the solution to the problem of self and society is romantic moralism.

"Down these mean streets a man must go who is not himself mean, who is neither tarnished nor afraid," goes Chandler's famous formula. "He must be the best man in his world and a good enough man for any world." The kind of detective fiction that Hugo loved to read was, we could say, about the possibility and illusion of being good. Hugo told his friends that he wrote a detective novel to help meet oncoming college tuition bills, but I think he wrote the book because central preoccupations in the genre rhymed with his own obsessions, and that we can usefully illuminate Hugo's achievement as a poet by examining those rhymes.

The axe murders that begin *Death and the Good Life* take place in Montana. The victims are killed outdoors, which means in Montana some of the things that "streets" mean in cities: where nobody knows who you are or where you came from, and where you're thrown back on your deepest habits of closing and disclosing your life to others, and to yourself. Bars are like this, too, and they figure prominently in the action of Hugo's book. Hugo's detective, Al "Mush Heart" Barnes, solves the first five murders early on, and while doing so he drinks with a 6'4" suspect in a hotel bar in a small Montana town.

> Swell detective. I was out with the number-one suspect in five axe killings, and I was getting drunk. That, I said to myself, is not only dumb, it is dangerous. . . . She seemed about as drunk as Billy Graham.

Self-deprecating wit is a feature of the genre perfected by Chandler. Here's Marlow in *Farewell, My Lovely:*

> I wasn't wearing a gun. . . I doubted if it would do me any good. The big man would probably take it away from me and eat it.

But what interests me here is not that Hugo would follow the conventions of the genre—Hugo was shrewd enough not to throw out anything useful when writing his only detective novel—but how he uses the conventions to infuse his book with what readers of his poetry will recognize as a characteristic vision.

About the axe murderer, "the psychiatrist's preliminary report had phrases about the psycho-dynamics of repeated anger and humiliation. . . ." Hugo's poems abound with those who have been degraded, shamed, humiliated, who have internalized the bad luck of their lives, and the bad choices, and the easy snobbery of others for whom smooth surfaces and gentility are signals of virtue. When Hugo's characters are drunk, anyone sober seems a type of Billy Graham: rhetorical, finger raised in denunciation and emphasis, smug, emotionally stingy, but for all this seemingly a better person because palpably sober.

The rest of the book's murders lead Barnes to Portland,

40

and the snarl of guilt and covering-up goes back twenty years, or a whole generation. The axe-murderer has a cruel, rigid father whom she can't please, hate directly, or get away from. And the murderers whom Barnes uncovers in Portland, in the book's second spree of guilt and murder, are living out a drama fixed in a familial past. This second plot is reminiscent of many Ross Macdonald plots, in which a family secret becomes, over a generation, motive for terrible deceit and violence, a shame and an anger both, a covenant. In Macdonald's books the secret often originates in the Midwest, and the consequences are lived out in California, at the end of the continent. Macdonald came from the Midwest to write his novels of flight, unravelling disguise and lurid family secrecy.

Hugo went to Montana from Seattle, his birthplace; his detective, Al Barnes, left the Seattle police force for Montana, for a good life, quiet and less murderous. Barnes is drawn back, to Portland rather than Seattle, but that fact matters less than that he is drawn back to a city, to a shameful past and a murderous present and the link between them. So that in Hugo's book, like so many of Macdonald's novels, the detective can't relax, can't forget what in the past he hoped to leave behind, but is driven by curiosity, sympathy, and professional pride to investigate again and again the link between something horribly wrong in the present and some source in the past which the guilty hope equally to conceal and to reenact.

The requirements of the genre present an interesting chore for the writer of detective fiction, and it is a characteristic of true artists that they make chores into opportunities. The chore is this: the identity and psychology of the murderer, the guilty one, must be both concealed and revealed. Part of the superficial appeal of the genre is that of puzzle-solving, and the puzzle must not be too easy nor must it be unfairly hard. The spine of the narrative—who is the killer and why?—must be hidden in its richly distracting surroundings, like a figure in a carpet, and also must be coherent and available, with no clues left out.

In other words, the book must want equally to cover and uncover its secret, and in this way the book is like the murderer, who wants with equal ferocity to hide and to tell the story of his life, and whose ambivalence on this very point is always the smolder in his psyche that makes him, to a sympathetic detective, discoverable.

We are near a crucial psychological fact about detective fiction now: the book is like the criminal, and the writer is like the detective.

Perhaps this understanding explains why so much detective fiction seems chilly, mechanical, like a technocrat's skill. The danger of the genre, for the writer, is that he or she will be so persuaded by the natural identity between the detective and the writer that the criminal naturally seems less good, less interesting, and, finally, the occasion for, once again, a proved superiority. The criminal becomes an object, like a finished book, a made thing, a chore expressed, pushed out of the self, both done and done for.

"Mush Heart" is Hugo's joke, but a serious one. The cop who cares about criminals and knows that he is guilty, too, though of crucially different things, needs to keep his improvised courage up, so he makes jokes about himself while getting drunk too fast with a 6'4" man-hating homicidal maniac woman of great conventional beauty who plans to seduce him and then slash his skull again and again with an axe. She used thirty-seven fury-fueled strokes on one victim.

> The sensuality in her face had been replaced by a cruelty that I found exciting. I found it sexually exciting, and I found it exciting because I believed I was really with a killer. I was drunk enough to be unable to sort out the two excitements. I was sure I would not have found her sexually exciting were I sober. But I wasn't sober.

Here "drunk" is a metaphor for an inability to sort out conflicting emotions. The plot of the novel gives Hugo an emotional truth to work with: if Barnes fails to distinguish between his job, which requires him to make discriminations, and his erotic ability to imagine the power and shape of the secret lives of others (full, like popular fiction, of sex and violence) by a potentially will-deadening sympathy, he will be hacked horribly to bits. But if Barnes fails to hesitate, to see the allure of both paths and to make jokes about how ridiculous and dangerous it is to allow his inner life full play, he will cease in some fatal way to be Barnes, who is after all a figure for an author whose killers are not only sympathetic but sexy, and abhorrent for all of that, because they are killers, as Barnes might have to be, in the line of plot and duty.

It is Hugo's ability to invest himself equally in his detective and his killers that makes *Death and the Good Life* (the title itself has a similar power of accommodation) of more than casual interest as an example of its genre, and that reminds us of his powers as a poet.

In *The Triggering Town*, a book of lectures and essays on poetry and writing, Hugo talks about public and private poets.

> The distinction lies in the relation of the poet to the language. With the public poet the intellectual and emotional contents of the words are the same for the reader as for the writer. With the private poet . . . the words, at least certain key words, mean something to the poet they don't mean to the reader.

Here's a list of such key words for Hugo: *grey, wind, shame, jokes, music, fail, river, degraded, warm*. We could begin to weave these together, like police trying to make a psychological profile of a suspect, but we will miss the force of the central obsession, the unity of the list that cannot be named because it is the undiscovered story behind the clues. If the poet knew it and could tell it, he wouldn't need the clues and we wouldn't have them. Elsewhere in *The Triggering Town* Hugo advises young writers as follows:

> . . . when you are writing you must assume that the next thing you put down belongs not for reasons of logic, good sense, or narrative development, but because you put it there. You, the same person who said that, also said this. The adhesive force is your way of writing, not sensible connection.

There are words on Hugo's list—*wind, river, jokes, music*—that connect us to time and to others, and words on the list—*shame, fail, degraded*—that make us stunned and inward. I think that *grey* and *warm* work both ways in Hugo's poems. They describe climate, emotional tone, and when combined they describe a "sad and humane" interior landscape, the one Hugo saw, I imagine, when he spent long hours "staring moodily out the window," as he often said to friends, never changing the phrase.

Warm refers to emotional honesty and responsibility, but it also refers to familiar isolating hypnotisms: drink, staring out windows, the presence of a story you can't tell.

Grey refers to the meld of isolation and connection, desire and experience, the contrasting black and white of print and judgment. And it means an imaginative opportunity: there are degrees of grey in Philipsburg, and Hugo was the man to invent the town in order to invent the poem in which he could distinguish among them, those degrees, holding lovingly and rejecting lovingly the old excuses:

> . . . Are magnesium
> and scorn sufficient to support a town,
> not just Philipsburg, but towns
> of towering blondes, good jazz and booze
> the world would never let you have
> until the town you came from dies inside?

Of course the town you came from never dies inside; to kill it or to let it die is to die yourself. Here's the beginning of "What Thou Lovest Well Remains American":

> You remember the name was Jensen. She seemed old
> always alone inside, face pasted gray to the window,
> and mail never came. Two blocks down, the Grubskis
> went insane. George played rotten trombone
> Easter when they flew the flag. Wild roses
> remind you the roads were gravel and vacant lots
> the rule. Poverty was real, wallet and spirit,
> and each day slow as church. You remember threadbare
> church groups on the corner, howling their faith
> at stars, and the violent Holy Rollers
> renting that barn for their annual violent sing
> and the barn burned down when you came back from war. . . .

The axe-murderer doesn't exist who can make this town die inside any of its children. The poem continues like this:

> Knowing the people you knew then are dead,
> you try to believe these roads are improved,
> the neighbors, moved in while you were away, good-looking,
> their dogs well fed. You still have need
> to remember lots empty and fern.
> Lawns well trimmed remind you of the train
> your wife took one day forever, some far empty town,
> the odd name you never recall. The time: 6:23.
> The day: October 9. The year remains a blur.
> You blame this neighborhood for your failure.
> In some vague way, the Grubskis degraded you
> beyond repair. And you know you must play again
> and again Mrs. Jensen at her window, must hear
> the foul music over the good slide of traffic.
> You loved them well and they remain, still with nothing
> to do, no money and no will. Loved them, and the gray
> that was their disease you carry for extra food
> in case you're stranded in some odd empty town
> and need hungry lovers for friends, and need feel
> you are welcome in the secret club they have formed.

The relationship between *need* and *secret* at the end of the poem is the very nub of what distinguishes a Ross Macdonald mystery plot from that of an ingenious artisan in the genre who is the helpless master of the genre's conventions but cannot weld them to a secret emotional plot about need, met or unmet.

Hugo has a chapter in *The Triggering Town* called "Assumptions." Earlier in the book he writes about the need a poet has for an ostensible subject, a pretext, an excuse for talking. "Writing off the Subject," he calls this essay.

> I suspect that the true or valid triggering subject is one in which physical characteristics or details correspond to attitudes the poet has toward the world or himself. For me, a small town that has seen better days works.

In his "Assumptions" chapter, Hugo describes such a town, and how he does or doesn't fit into it. Sometimes the descriptions are logically contradictory but emotionally consistent, as in this sequence of three assumptions:

The churches are always empty.

A few people attend church and the sermons are boring.

Everybody but me goes to church and the sermons are inspiring.

Here are two contiguous items later in the chapter.

No crime.

A series of brutal murders took place years ago. The murderer was never caught and is assumed still living in town.

A town in which anyone might be an undiscovered murderer is a radical psychological and spiritual disorder, and in traditional British murder fiction the community—the vicarage, the country estate, the grand hotel—is restored to social order by the discovery of the murderer's identity.

But the restored order in the American detective novel is different. It's personal order that's at stake, and primarily or wholly the detective's—an interior order, a sort of personal visionary calm, the possibility of being good revived after the novel's long slog through murk and violence. Being interior, it is hard to describe, and so is often symbolized by physical calm or comfort—a relaxed time in a beautiful landscape, food and drink with friends, small ceremonies of comfort and ease.

Hugo's poem "High Grass Prairie" works similarly.

> Say something warm. Hello. This world
> was full of harm until this wind
> placated grass and put the fish to rest.
> And wave hello. Someone may be out there
> riding undulating light our way.
> Wherever we live, we sleep here
> where cattle sleep beside the full canal.
> We slept here young in poems.

The canal runs on without us east
a long flow into Fairfield. The grass flows
ever to us, ever away, the way it did
that war we dreamed this land alive.
The man we hoped was out there
saw our signal and is on the way.
Say something warm. Hello. You can sleep
forever in this grass and not be cold.

Murder in the American detective novel rises so often from
bitterness and secrecy and degradation and shame that mur-
der itself, horrible as it is, seems more nearly a symptom than
a disease. The best detectives in the genre (Spade, Marlow,
Archer) recognize murderous emotions from the pressures of
their own lives but express such pressure differently from
murderers because the detectives have a code of behavior to
live by. Their relationship to Hemingway heroes has been
widely noted. It's the other meaning of "code" that interests
me here; the detective is like Hugo's private poet, one for
whom "words, at least certain key words, mean something to
the poet they don't mean to the reader."

For the detective, too, has a secret—as much as the mur-
derer he is in agonized possession of something he lives by,
something of more value to him than anything else in his life,
and he is therefore torn whether to reveal or conceal it. To the
extent, I think, that the writer understands this situation to be
true for both his detective and his murderer, the writer grows
more vividly human and less mechanical even when working
in a constricted and highly formulaic genre. Understanding
the link between detective and murderer to be a link, finally,
in his own psyche, the writer is able to prevent himself from
identifying too largely with the detective.

None of the best workers in the genre has been free, nor
has wanted to be, from the temptation in Chandler's formula,
to create a detective who is "the best man in his world." But
the best workers have become the best by struggling with the
need for their murderers to be as loveable as they are mon-
strous; indeed, the balance between those two attributes may
be the narrative's reflection of the writer's struggle with the

urge, on the one hand, to create and rule their books at whatever cost (in this they are like their murderers), and on the other hand, to effect an aesthetic balance and a pleasing calm, to distribute themselves pantheistically throughout the narrative (and in this they are like their detectives, restorers of inner balance).

Hugo's immense empathetic abilities are at the center of his imagination. "Someone may be out there / riding undulating light our way," he imagines. In popular art (I'm thinking of *Close Encounters of the Third Kind* and *E.T.*) the one who welcomes the space people has to be a child, an unstructured innocence. What the hell, the space people may not even be people. The eventually sympathetic doctor played by Peter Coyote in *E.T.* can be *seen* overcoming his adult experience in order to have, as the phrase goes, a heart. He overcomes his adult experience at approximately the same rate the audience weeps as it accepts the film's invitation to lament aging.

But if I could choose who to meet a spaceship, with what sort of hopefulness, it would be Richard Hugo rather than Eliot, the boy in the film. Hugo's vision is nostalgic, too, but the nostalgia of a man Hugo's age (fifty-eight when he died) has more accumulation than Eliot's. He has more home to long for.

The title poem of *White Center* (it refers, among other things, to a drab section of West Seattle) describes these mean streets.

> Town or poem, I don't care how it looks. Old woman
> take my hand and we'll walk one more time these streets
> I believed marked me weak beneath catcalling clouds.
> Long ago, the swamp behind the single row of stores
> was filled and seeded. Roses today where Toughy Hassin
> slapped my face to the grinning delight of his gang.
> I didn't cry or run. Had I fought him
> I'd have been beaten and come home bloody in tears
> and you'd have told me I shouldn't be fighting.
>
> Wasn't it all degrading, mean Mr. Kyle sweeping
> the streets for no pay, believing what he'd learned
> as a boy in England: "This is your community"?

I taunted him to rage, then ran. Is this the day
we call bad mothers out of the taverns and point them
sobbing for home, or issue costumes to posturing clowns
in the streets, make fun of drunk barbers, and hope
someone who left and made it returns, vowed
to buy more neon and give those people some class?

The Dugans aren't worth a dime, dirty Irish, nor days
you offered a penny for every fly I killed.
You were blind to my cheating. I saw my future certain—
that drunk who lived across the street and fell
in our garden reaching for the hoe you dropped.
All he got was our laughter. I helped him often home
when you weren't looking. I loved some terrible way
he lived in his mind and tried to be decent to others.
I loved the way we loved him behind our disdain.

Clouds. What glorious floating. They always move on
like I should have early. But your odd love and a war
taught me the world's gone evil past the first check point
and that's First Avenue South. I fell asleep each night
safe in love with my murder. The neighbor girl
plotted to tease me every tomorrow and watch me turn
again to the woods and games too young for my age.
We could never account for the python cousin Warren
found half starved in the basement of Safeway.

It all comes back but in bites. I am the man
you beat to perversion. That was the drugstore MacCameron
flipped out in early one morning, waltzing
on his soda fountain. The siren married his shrieking.
His wife said, "We'll try again, in Des Moines."
You drove a better man into himself where he found tunes
he had no need to share. It's all beginning to blur
as it forms. Men cracking up or retreating.
Resolute women deep in hard prayer.

And it isn't the same this time. I hoped forty years
I'd write and would not write this poem. This time would die
and your grave never reopen. Or mine. Because I'm married
and happy, and across the street a foster child
from a cruel past is safe and need no longer crawl
for his meals, I walk this past with you, ghost in any field
of good crops certain I remember everything wrong.

If not, why is this road lined with fern
and why do I feel no shame kicking the loose gravel home.

Whoever this woman is—if not the poet's mother, then any-
one's ("Is this the day / we call bad mothers out of the
taverns. . . ?")—the ferocity behind the slap of the poem
should sting forever. "I am the man / you beat to perver-
sion . . ." is an accusation, though it's not clear of whom, nor if
perversion doesn't apply to both people here. The line-
break's recall of Whitman's testimonial and witnessing mode
is surely intentional: Hugo hopes to speak to us all, and in
some way for us all.

Another line-break to note: "I loved some terrible way / he
lived in his mind and tried to be decent to others."

But the lines I want to end by citing are these: "I fell asleep
each night / safe in love with my murder." Surely these lines
refer to that condition of empathetic evenhandedness that I
suggest is the requisite of a good detective novel, since only
such an achievement can make visible through the conven-
tional school figures of the genre the radical moral dilemma
that is the genre's secret, which the genre struggles equally to
conceal and reveal: one must love the murderer and the detec-
tive equally, and one must be everyone in the book, even the
murdered.

For Hugo, I imagine, the sleep of the just was not sought;
on the evidence of his poems I imagine that justice seemed to
him both a beautiful impossibility and a necessary joke. It is
conventional for fictional American detectives to be troubled
sleepers and insomniacs. No wonder, if their work is to get, as
only a powerful poet could, a syntax to sleep in which would
organize "safe" and "love" and "murder."

(1985)

Merida, 1969
for Russell Banks

We sat in the courtyard
like landlords and dispatched
teak-colored Manolo
at intervals for Carta Blanca,
and propped idiomatically
little wedges of lime on top
of the bottles like party hats.
O tristes tropiques. Our pretty
wives were sad and so were we.
So this is how one lives when he
is sad, we almost said out loud.
Manolo, we cried, and his tough
feet came skittering across
the blue, rain-streaked tiles.

Travel turned out to be no
anodyne, for we went home.
It was a sort of metaphor,
we now agree, a training
in loss. For if we'd been happy
then, as now we often are,
we'd have sat there in Merida
with its skyline of churchspires
and windmills, the latter
looking like big tin dande-
lions from which the fluff
had just been blown by wind
they couldn't hold, and we'd cry
Manolo, and beer would arrive.

I was first stirred to write "Merida, 1969," by looking at a watercolor of Merida used as the cover illustration for Elizabeth Bishop's *The Complete Poems 1927–1979*. Miss Bishop herself did the drawing. I had been in Merida some fifteen years ago; an old friend, the novelist Russell Banks, and I had spent a week there with our wives, now our ex-wives. And Banks was about to arrive in Maine, where I wrote the poem, for a visit, and so I had been thinking about friendship, its duration, the mutual stories friends invent and revise. And since Banks had recently remarried and I would soon remarry, I was prickly, sentimental, skeptical, alert. In short I was about to start work on a poem, and had a welter of musings, memories, notions, and confusions to work with.

Miss Bishop's drawing is dated (1942) and perhaps that's why my title includes a date, though I may in any case have wanted to set the time and place quickly in the title. Probably there were in draft some lines that I had to write and reject before I found my first line; I no longer have any version of the poem but the one given here.

One thing I know about the form the poem took is that I didn't decide on it before I started work, as I sometimes do, nor did I assume the poem would find a form on behalf of its own urgencies, as I sometimes do. What I must have wanted was for the poem to hint at some possibilities from which I could choose some constraints, but not until I was a little way into the poem and could sense what manner of resistance (4 ohms? 8 ohms?) might serve it best.

What I wound up with was a sort of mirrored diptych, two fourteen-line stanzas, one recounting 1969 and one about knowledge in the present, one narrative and one reflective, each one using some of the same incidents and atmosphere. There would be an implied contrast, naturally enough. How much has changed in the interval? How much have we learned? If we knew then what we know now . . . ?

Of course the preceding paragraph is written with hindsight, rather than with the attentive bumbling and diligent indolence that accompany composition. What I remember about writing the poem is that somewhere about five or six lines along I sensed, the way people suddenly know what it is they would like to eat for lunch, that I'd like the stanza to be fourteen lines, that in the blank space between the two stanzas—yes, there should be two stanzas—there would be an invisible hinge, and that the poem could propose by such a form an implied relationship between the past and the present that the poem could question and doubt.

Probably Frost's "The Road Not Taken" is a sort of model for my poem, though on a sufficiently unconscious level that I had no thought of it or of Frost while I was writing. We all remember the ending of that poem:

> I shall be telling this with a sigh
> Somewhere ages and ages hence:
> Two roads diverged in a wood, and I—
> I took the one less traveled by,
> And that has made all the difference.

We sometimes forget how differently the poem's speaker describes the two roads at the time he actually chose one of them.

> . . . long I stood
> And looked down one as far as I could
> To where it bent in the undergrowth;
>
> Then took the other, as just as fair,
> And having perhaps the better claim,
> Because it was grassy and wanted wear;
> Though as for that the passing there
> Had worn them really about the same,
>
> And both that morning equally lay
> In leaves no step had trodden black.
> Oh, I kept the first for another day!
> Yet knowing how way leads on to way,
> I doubted if I should ever come back.

The roads beckoned about the same, but later, when the pleasure of telling the story was part of the story's truth, and there was much intervening life to explain, we could hear the poem's speaker veer off again, this time away from incident and toward shapeliness.

> Two roads diverged in a wood, and I—
> I took the one less traveled by,
> And that has made all the difference.

"And I," he says, pausing for dramatic effect and then giving his little anecdote a neat and summary dramatic effect that's in the story but not in the original event. Though of course by this stage in the life of the story each exists somewhat for the sake of the other.

My friend, an able writer of stories, was coming to visit, and one of the things I was mulling was how stories work.

Fourteen lines was no accident. I've written a number of pale sonnets, unrhymed and in a trimeter or tetrameter line that hovers somewhere between so-called free verse and metrically regular verse. It's a territory I've been attracted to by noticing how the two modes, so often poised against each other in neat and false opposition, want to be each other. Be that as it may, I've had happy experience with fourteen-line poems, and so poising two stanzas that length against each other, in ways I had yet to work out, satisfied both my need for familiarity and my need for surprise. With luck, then, the poem had a form to become, and I had both the comforts and challenges of an apt form. . . .

How well this all turned out the reader may judge. The two friends in my poem seem to behave about the same under either disposition—the narrative past, in the first stanza, or the past as understood along all the intervening time, in the second. In this second and hypothetical life, they may or may not be wiser, but they are happier, and manifest their happiness, as they did in 1969, by sending for beer. And why not? How often do we get a chance to vacation like this? Won't it all seem like a dream in, say, fifteen years?

The equality of the two behaviors is at least made easier—and perhaps made possible, for all I know now, long after I wrote the poem—by the discovery of the form.

What else should I say about the form? Content is often unsettling or painful in poems, but form is play, a residue of the fun the poet had while working. Of course, like form and content, pain and fun want to be each other. . . .

(1987)

On Stanley Plumly's *Summer Celestial*

The poems in Stanley Plumly's *Summer Celestial* are so thoroughly composed, so beautifully realized, that they seem to offer us not only themselves, but also sure ways to read and know them.

As much as his preceding book, *Out-of-the-Body Travel* (1977), was organized by a powerful antagonism between the poet and his father, *Summer Celestial* is a book laved by the poet's love for his mother. Many of the poems are set in the poet's childhood, and so to read this book like Plumly's last one in terms of family drama makes common sense.

Another way to read Plumly is as a kind of Ohio Wordsworthian. The book's first poem, "Tree Ferns," has a small boy cut with a pocketknife a length of "the local Ohio palm," as if to have in advance a token of the manhood from which Plumly's poems so lovingly recreate boyhood, finding the twig in the tree and the child in the adult, "cutting and whittling them down" until they fit into these poems.

A central poem in *Summer Celestial* is "My Mother's Feet." I mean, of course, that it's emotionally central, and it occupies page 26 of a fifty-two page collection.

> How no shoe fit them,
> and how she used to prop them,
> having dressed for bed,
> letting the fire in the coal-stove blue
>
> and blink out, falling asleep in her chair.
> How she bathed and dried them, night after night,
> and rubbed their soreness like an intimacy.
> How she let the fire pull her soft body through them.

The poem begins in midstride, in a fairy-tale thrall: there's no slipper for this Cinderella. The feet take on the cooling blue of the fire; the ceremony is a change of sentries. This Christ washes Her own feet in order that Her lambs may sleep.

Because feet are where we meet the ground, they're like a membrane, the plane where energy turns to matter or vice versa. But to the mother these magical feet are just sore feet, and she gives them the abstracted attention we spend, for example, on kitchen utensils. It's the son who sees the hint of magic.

> She was the girl who grew just standing,
> the one the picture cut at the knees.
> She was the girl who seemed to be dancing
> out on the lawn, after supper, alone.
>
> I have watched her climb the militant stairs
> and down again, watched the ground go out from under her.
> I have seen her on the edge of chances—
> she fell, when she fell, like a girl.

The maiming "cut at the knees" is like the psychic violence inflicted on women who play too carefully the role of selfless wife and mother: they can't initiate actions, they serve, they just stand and wait. So it must be partly in compensation that the mother in Plumly's poem dances, or seems to dance, but only by herself and after the household is fed. There may be a suggestion here that the feet won't or can't be photographed, in protection of their magical properties, but if so the joke is on the feet: nobody wanted a picture of them anyhow. The magic and ignored feet are pack animals, drudges, takers of routine chances. What is talismanic in the mother that can be known by love of her feet—that those feet carry a dancing girl disguised as an exhausted wife and mother—is only visible to her son, to the poem's beholding I.

> Someone who loved her said she walked on water.
> Where there is no path nor wake. As a child
> I would rise in the half-dark of the house,
> from a bad dream or a noisy window,

something, almost, like snow in the air,
and wander until I could find those feet, propped
and warm as a bricklayer's hands,
every step of the way shining out of them.

They have no path or wake, just as they don't appear in photographs: they don't exist in the material world except as feet, but in the spiritual world of the poem they are like a grail or a magic stone. The son is going on a quest and needs to know the way. And the way leads home, where the heroic work to be done is to tell the story of the mother's feet, to redeem the girl in the poet's mother from the gift she has given him.

So far as that gift is light (so that the poet can wake to half-dark from membranes of another world, like dreams or windows, where he was terrified as a child), and so far as that gift is warmth, the poem is thanks. The gift is also dark, for by standing guard, as the phrase goes, the mother took care of light and let her son go into the dark of sleep to dream of quests.

And in that dark grows obligation. As much as the questing son may have thought to adventure in a large world and find something, he must return again and again to the first path lest something be lost, lest his mother's feet be taken for granted, mistaken for mere feet. The way shining out of them—the reader thinks, in a flicker, of those white and black feet in books explaining ballroom dancing—is a circle.

And so a kind of patio-Freudian reading of Plumly's work, that he is the most frankly Oedipal of our male poets, combines with a reading in which Wordsworth's influence lights much of Plumly's circular way.

"I think of how the old survive: we make them up," Plumly writes in "After Whistler," and in the same poem,

> Even the painter's mother is staring into the future,
> as if her son could paint her back into her body.

Or, "I'm remembering / how I knew I had a soul. . . ." Or,

> There is almost nothing that does not signal loneliness,
> Then loveliness, then something connecting all we will
> become.

But the poems in *Summer Celestial* are more emotionally complex than such readings suggest.

Summer Celestial has three sections, and the book's title poem closes the middle one. The poem is a kind of mutant sestina: it has seven seven-line stanzas. There are no recurring end words such as a sestina requires, though by the way the poem turns over and over in its hands central images and topics of the whole book, three words end lines twice: *money, sleep, back*. More than any of Plumly's earlier books, *Summer Celestial* has a core vocabulary. These words appear again and again in the poems, each time differently lit by their context. The effect both duplicates the ritual repetitions of obsession and the way we think ourselves out of obsession by dismantling into discreet and separable instances the brute and monolithic force of central recurring tropes.

Earlier Plumly poems—most notably "The Iron Lung," from *Out-of-the-Body Travel*—have worked by making a sort of narrative from words in the book's core vocabulary. It isn't a narrative that purports to happen in "real time," because it's not about events but about thought, and the form of thought it most resembles, because it is condensed, elliptical and highly self-referential, is dreaming. One way to describe the contrast between such poems and the more conventionally made poems in Plumly's books is by analogy, referring to the era in jazz history when improvisations began to be based more on chord changes than on melody. The effect is that the structure and the surface of the song are no longer easy to distinguish; the music seems to be about, to the extent that music is "about" anything, its own shaping principles.

One current theory of dreaming is that the higher brain is subjected to random bombardment from a "dream generator" in the brainstem, and that dreams are the result of the higher brain's attempt to weave from such vivid and discontinuous fragments a coherent, shapely story.

There is of course nothing random about Plumly's core vocabulary in *Summer Celestial*. The words in it bear recognizably the pressure of choice, though whether the poet chose them or they him is not always easy to guess. The words are *money, sleep, back, light, dust, dark, name, tree, mother, cold, water, dream, body.* We could make a penetrating reading of Plumly's book by treating each poem as an attempt to associate, from whatever starting point, as many of the words in the core vocabulary as possible, and to make from such association a coherent, shapely story.

By such a curiosity the dreamlike and hypnotic title poem is the book's most capacious.

> At dusk I row out to what looks like light or anonymity,
> too far from land to be called to, too close to be lost,
> and drag oar until I can drift in and out of a circle,
> the center of a circle, nothing named, nothing now to see,
> the wind up a little and down, building against the air,
> and listen to anything at all, bird or wind, or nothing
> but the first sounds on the surface, clarifying, clear.

The poem's second line gives a beautifully ambivalent poise: unreachable but not lost represents both a safe place and ("If it is true the soul is other people") a terrifying dilemma. It's almost like a preliminary to meditation: the conditions must be perfect, the location exact, the mind emptied. What will occur to one?

> Once, in Canada, I saw a man stand up in his boat and pass
> out dollar bills. It was summer dark. They blew down
> on the lake like moonlight. Coming out of his hands
> they looked like dollar bills. When I look up at the Dippers,
> the whole star chart, leaves on a tree, sometimes all night,
> I think about his balance over the cold water, under stars,
> standing in a shoe, the nets all down and gathering.

The shoe represents the first overt allusion in the poem to Winken, Blinken, and Nod. Aside from the sestina form itself, and the formal habits of dreams, the other strong organizational influence at work in the poem is the lulling repetitive force of children's literature and bedtime stories.

> My mother still wakes crying do I think she's made of money.
> —And what makes money make money make money?
> I wish I could tell her how to talk herself to sleep.

I wish. She says she's afraid she won't make it back.
As in a prayer, she is more afraid of loneliness than death.
Two pennies for the eyes, two cents: I wish I could tell her
that each day the stars reorganize, each night they come back
    new.

A penny for your thoughts. Two cents worth. You can't take it
with you. The poem is in a fury of association; it can use
almost any connection for its purposes. We might even say the
connections *are* its purposes. And the speaker is like a dreamer,
by now; he's both a character and a spectator. The boat is all the
boats that can be associated to it, and the night is both new and
all nights that memory and image can hold together.

Outside tonight the waters run to color with the sky.
In the old water dream you wake up in a boat, drifting out.
Everything is cold and smells of rain. Somewhere back there,
in sleep, you remember weeping. And at this moment you
    think
you are about to speak. But someone is holding on, hand
over hand, and someone with your voice opening and closing.
In water you think it will always be your face that floats
to the surface. . . .

There is loss, love is irremediably spent, and in grief one
returns to ritual safeties. But one is not alone (someone is
holding on), and one is not with the others.

You think it will always be your face that floats
to the surface. Flesh is on fire under water. The nets go back
to gather and regather, and bring up stones, viridian and
    silver,
what falls. In the story, the three Dutch fishermen sail out
for stars, into the daylight hours, so loaded with their catch
it spills. They sleep, believe it, where they can, and dry
their nets on a full moon. For my mother, who is afraid to
    sleep,
for anyone afraid of heights or water, all of this is intolerable.

The workmanlike and insouciant fishermen in their shoe
(how is this shoe related to the no shoe that fit the poet's

mother's feet?) become the emblem of art, of restoring work, of poise that is not stasis.

> Look, said the wish, into your lover's face. Mine over yours.
> In that other life, which I now commend to you, I have spent
> the days by a house along the shore, building a boat, tying
> the nets together, watching the lights go on and off on the water.
> But nothing gets done, none of it ever gets finished. So I lie down
> in a dream of money being passed from hand to hand in a long line.
> It looks like money—or hands taking hands, being led out to deeper water. . . .

"To need and the needs of others," another poem in *Summer Celestial* has it, and it will serve as one reading for deeper water. Others include the unconscious and the unknown, and the colloquial meanings of the phrase. And if the soul is other people, deeper water is the soul.

> to deeper water. I wake up weeping, and it is almost joy.
> I go outside and the sky is sea-blue, the way the earth is looked at
> from the moon. And out on the great surfaces, water is paying
> back water. I know, I know this is a day and the stars reiterate,
> return each loss, each witness. And that always in the room next door
> someone is coughing all night or a man and a woman make love,
> each body buoyed, even blessed, by what the other cannot have.

This spectacular poem takes place over a long insomniac night, and of course also over a lifetime. I suppose this kind of density and inclusiveness and balance are what is meant by the widely cited phrase, "the momentary peace of the poem."

Well, the poem is not momentary. But the poet and the book, in their different ways, go on.

Summer Celestial's third section contains ten astringent poems, compared to the musical amplitude and resolution of "Summer Celestial." The poet's mother is in only one of these poems, unless she appears again as one of the young girls at the end of the second section of "After Rilke":

> they will be mothers, year after year,
> and will sit at tables half in, half out of light,
> waiting for someone at the hour assigned
> in a room adjacent where they can be alone
> and be at peace and let themselves lie down in a long death,
> still married to need and the needs of others.

And Ohio is invoked in only one poem (though it is never far from the landscape of Plumly's poems, even those set in Virginia, his other boyhood home), about a heron in Maine that sets off memories of birds and rivers in Ohio.

> It rises in snow, white on white, the way
> in memory one thing is confused with another.

That snow appears in another poem in the third section. Snow is a kind of cold dust, the way "light . . . is the dust made whole." The poem is called "Snowing, Sometimes," and it begins with an echo of Plumly's wonderful poem "The Iron Lung."

> You couldn't keep it out.

A few lines later: "It was like dust, an elegance, / like frost." What *was* it? Well, it was snow, of course: the poem begins with snow and returns to snow. What else?

"Summer Celestial" embodies not only "the way / in memory one thing is confused with another"—the formulation is less than half-bad as a working definition of metaphor—but also the way that we're overloaded, flooded by our lives, and respond by making, in dream or in art, beautiful resolutions from what in a life without art or dreaming would be nearly fatal ambivalences.

The poems in the third section of *Summer Celestial*, for

which in this brief essay "Snowing, Sometimes" will have to stand as representative, address not the transforming power of the imagination, but that which we cannot transform, whether because it is outside our power to transform it or because we choose not to try to transform it. Here are the poem's last three stanzas.

> If you fell asleep you knew
> it could cover you, cover you
> the way cold closes on water.
> It would shine, like ice,
> inside you. If you woke up
> early, the cup on the bureau
> cracked, you were sure that
> even the pockets of your pants,
> hung on the back of the chair,
> would be filled. Nothing could
> stop it, could keep it out.

> Not the room in sunlight, nor
> smoky with the rain. Not
> the mother sweeping, nor
> building the woodfire each
> morning. Not the wind blowing
> backwards, without sound.
> Not the boy at the window
> who loves the look of it
> dusting the ground, whiter
> than flour, piled in the

> small, far corners.

What seems to me most powerful and harrowing in *Summer Celestial* is the struggle between the inclusive, linking, harmonizing impulses of the title poem—which moves by its formal authority toward the power music has to persuade without raising the question of assent—on the one hand, and on the other hand the leaner and more antiseptic impulses of poems like "Snowing, Sometimes," which isolate, question, and define what in Plumly's other mode would be folded into a larger poise.

This struggle drives Plumly's poems like a heart. Probably

it is a life's work. Most poets whose urgencies are as profoundly autobiographical as Plumly's lack either his transforming powers or his distrust of those powers, and so their unmediated reliance on autobiography causes their later work to run out of subject matter, steam, or both. No fate seems less likely for Plumly, and few bodies of work—a handful or two—in his generation seem as likely to reward our continuing, excited attention.

(1984)

Dishonesty and Bad Manners

In his foreword to *Collected Shorter Poems 1927–1957,* Auden wrote

> A dishonest poem is one which expresses, no matter how well, feelings or beliefs which its author never felt or entertained.

He also defines (Auden was an addicted definer) bad-mannered poems.

> In art as in life, bad manners, not to be confused with a deliberate attempt to cause offence, are the consequence of an over-concern with one's own ego and a lack of consideration for (and knowledge of) others. Readers, like friends, must not be shouted at or treated with brash familiarity. Youth may be forgiven when it is brash or noisy, but this does not mean that brashness and noise are virtues.

Auden is writing about keeping a civil tongue in your head, especially if you're a poet, and because he is the least Romantic and most disintoxicating of our important poets, and the most concerned with civic and social themes, he provides useful texts for thinking about writing not as a solitary rapture of the desk, but as a civic and social activity and thereby subject to the moral vocabulary we use to describe and puzzle over our common lives.

Because I'm interested in a literary question here, though not in literary name-calling, the examples I use will be two poems from my own first book, *Ruining the New Road* (1970). The first is called "The Asian War."

We talk about it
clinically, as if it were
a mold the body couldn't
shed. We've lost control.
Our fingers thicken,
growing a hot clumsy crust
until they are as stiff
as icicles and we drop
everything, leaflets,
bombs, all hope.

Two suspect features of the poem are the disparity between its modest size and the scope its title promises, and the knowing use of the pronoun "we," which only rings emotionally true, to my present ears, in the sentence "We've lost control."

The image of the body both incompetent and ill refers to the body politic. We all belong to that, so to speak in the first person plural isn't, by itself, foolish. But the poem implies a diagnosis: that clinical speech may be inappropriate. And another: that the war is not an action but a disease that causes actions.

The first diagnosis is surely open to debate and the second is a textbook example of circular argument. In each case, the "we" seems presumptuous.

As political analysis, the poem has the serious disadvantage of depicting a hopeless situation. The war is given as a sort of bad dream that the body politic acts out, rationalizing its behavior ("We talk about it / clinically"), but helplessly impelled ("We've lost control") to that behavior.

If the poem had not hoped to ward off its confusion and despair by offering analysis, but had instead offered a clearer description of its confusion and despair—saying, in effect, how it felt without hoping to say why—I'd not think it a wonderful poem but I wouldn't complain about it in the moral vocabulary I've used here. And crucial to the difference between the two strategies is the choice between "I" and "we."

As for the title, it might have well been something more documentary and specific. "Listening to Radio News of the Vietnam War," for example. To call it the "Asian" war refers to a political theory more than to the war. Those of us who opposed the war had our domino theory, too.

The failures the poem embodies are not worth much breast-beating, after all. I was hardly the only American to be so hurt and confused by the war itself and its deep impact on domestic politics that I wanted to have a more coherent explanation for my pain than I could, in fact, manage.

But a poem of honest muddle would have been more useful to me, and to any readers the poem might attract.

Auden's weakness as a critic, and arguably one cause of the lapse of quality in his late poems, is encapsulated by his phrase, "in art as in life."

The most Horatian of modern poets, Auden understood decorum in poetry more or less as Horace did, and thus deserves, by association, Petronius's praising tag, *curiosa felicitas*, studied felicity. The phrase could as easily describe the poet (life) as his work (art).

But decorum is different in life than in art; one brings different freedoms and responsibilities than the other. Certain white lies and social lies, for example, are crucial to social life, but even small mendacities about one's feelings are poison to a poem. In life the "truth" is usually braided complicatedly with the "facts," but in art invention can be truth's Hermes.

There are two decorums here, and maybe a third that governs negotiations between the two I've described. In either case, the situation is more complicated than Auden described.

It should be a commonplace that love poems raise questions of honesty and matters at least as readily as political poems. As I did with "The Asian War," I'll begin worrying about "Our Song" by thinking about pronouns: who's speaking, to whom, why, and about what?

Here's the poem.

> And when you shake your colonies of hair,
> you are a willow of bellropes.
> All who have loved you clang:
> a treeful of musical bruises.
> It gives you something to hum,
> an anthem, falling asleep.

This poem too is probably too short. In the absence of narrative or circumstantial values, it's hard to know what's going on and what's at stake.

Mind you, I make no brief for narrative or circumstantial values in and of themselves. The burgeoning theoretical interest in narrative poetry seems to me spilt religion. Things happen consecutively in narrative that happen simultaneously in psychic life, and there are many critics and poets who prefer the experience of consecutive time to simultaneous time because it makes moral discourse easier, and because causality and guilt are easier to assert as religious or quasi-religious principles in narrative than in any of the many other experiences of time.

But this poem is all metaphor and tone, all implication. It's like a tiny gothic without even a tiny house.

It has a small clump of political images (*colonies, anthem*) and a larger cluster of musical ones (*anthem, music, hum, clang, bellropes*). *Hair* and *willow* are related, and perhaps to *falling*. It's possible that *shake, bruises,* and *asleep* are related.

But the poem won't tell us how.

There may be issues of sexual jealousy afoot ("all who have loved you"), and the woman, asleep, may be like another country, which would enliven *anthem* and *colonies*. But who is bruised? Why is the title "our" song rather than the woman's, or for that matter the speaker's? I suppose the title could be ironic, but it's hard to be ironic about something so ill-defined as the emotional field of this poem. Questions abound.

My guess is that it's a fearful poem, and that, like "The Asian War," it falls into its incoherence precisely because it longs so fiercely for coherence, because it wants to be knowing. "Ineptitude," Flaubert concluded, "consists in wanting to reach conclusions."

I want, of course, to make it clear that I'm not writing in contempt of these poems. They're not good, but the mistakes I made in them have been instructive to me. I'd rather not have collected them in a book, but I didn't know any better then. Anyhow, I have real affection for the youth in which I wrote them, and some of that glow spills over them.

As for the silly things we've all said and written, we should bear in mind Lichtenberg's dictum: "One must judge men, not by their opinions, but by what their opinions have made of them." Women, too.

The problem, at least in my two poems, is not that the young are noisy and brash, though God knows I knew how to be both. Noise and brashness may merely be prerogatives of the young, just as shushing and correcting the young are prerogatives of the old.

Both the moral and social imperatives the title of this brief essay refers to are satisfied, or not, at a private level of self-confrontation that exists previous to any question of decorum. A poet has to be willing to be honestly confused and honestly fearful, and not to make a poem as a charm against confusion and fear. Everyone who teaches or studies the writing of poetry knows Valéry's aphorism: "A poem is never finished, only abandoned." But there are plenty of unfinished poems.

I might better call them unstarted poems. It's not clear how, in Auden's definition of a dishonest poem, anybody but the poet could make real use of the term, for only the poet knows what feelings or beliefs he or she has never felt or entertained. And of course the poet doesn't always know that, who doesn't always know what's felt until it's said.

What I mean by an unstarted poem is a charm against confusion and fear. It's as if a chef assembled all the ingredients and implements to make a dish and then cried out, "Voila! I know how to make this," and then walked away. In the case of the two poems I've cited here, that's what I did. It was a case, no doubt, of almost too much feeling, rather than of feelings that I'd never felt.

As for bad manners, it would surely be a mistake for me to apologize a second time for publishing them. Tact for a reader is even easier. If an unstarted poem comes across your path, you just lower your eyes and let it go by.

(1980)

Cameo Roles

Ten years ago, I read in Stevens's essay "The Noble Rider and the Sound of Words" his description of the poet's role.

> I think that his function is to make his imagination theirs and that he fulfills himself only as he sees his imagination become the light in the minds of others. His role, in short, is to help people to live their lives.

Writing poems seemed so socially useless and therefore selfish a preoccupation that I liked the altruistic lilt of that latter sentence. I was too young and dull to sense how complicated a notion it was for Stevens, how his ringing assertion of it rode too smoothly over the difficulties the idea gave him, and how lucidly practical an idea it was: that since we live our lives in great part by imagining them, we had better do it well. I was too young and dull for Stevens in general, much less in specific. And some of the points he made I resisted: we not only want our youths but we want the delusions of youth and the fun of casting them off. So what he wrote, that "after all, the noble style, in whatever it creates, merely perpetuates the noble style," I contrived to read quickly. I liked the noble style and thought it might fit me one of these fine days.

Less dull and less young, I daily find myself more grateful for Stevens, not only for the vast and wonderful body of his poems, but for his confrontation—the smartest, strangest, and most direct I know—with the question of how to live. Once I couldn't imagine that. I thought him a dandy, and fearfully abstract.

The noble style I had in mind was more characteristically

American. Lincoln would do, or even Adlai Stevenson, whom I watched from the waft of my mother's admiration for him: he addressed a few of us from the rear of a train in 1952 in Troy, Ohio, and then chugged nobly off to Piqua. He was something. Stevens was confusing. Adlai Stevenson was the first hero I shared with an adult. Stevens wouldn't stand still, and I was looking for the wrong effect anyway.

> But as a wave is a force and not the water of which it is composed, which is never the same, so nobility is a force and not the manifestations of which it is composed, which are never the same.

Here the noble style, I imagine, would indulge itself in a figure: a pair of railroad tracks. The noble style would not be so crude as to say so, but they represent "imagination" and "reality," and with the help of perspective they perform the easy, paradoxical stunt railroad tracks are famous for. The noble style loves recurrences, and so Adlai Stevenson, gracefully and ironically the moral straight man of this figure, would reappear. Not in my little tribute, in which Stevenson performs a cameo role and worries off to Piqua forever, a man with the wrong ambitions and smart enough to know it. That trope about the railroad tracks is too easy, he's thinking. He's right. He's my noble rider, whom each hero-worshipper dooms never to dismount, and so I leave him dark-browed on memory's side of Piqua, where I can keep sentimental track of him any time I like.

To Stevens, as I slowly grow less dull and rapidly grow less young, I give something rare, at least for me. Adlai Stevenson I have converted, like a true fan, to an event in my biography. But I have tried to make myself an event in Stevens's biography. He wanted to be a light in the mind of others, he says. I don't know how he came to feel about that sentence, first published in 1942. Once you consider, as I do here, what happens in the minds of others to that ambition, you see how what is most noble in the urge won't work. The poet wants not to express himself, not to make the imaginations of others his, but "to make his imagination theirs." He wants to accommodate himself. He is fearful of his own imaginative powers, which may be merely fanciful. His powers need resistance and so seek to clang against the solidity of others, whose perversity is guard against his own.

This plan would work splendidly except that these solid and perverse citizens are busy replacing the pictures on the walls and cooking food they hate but imagine he loves. Like me, they want his light in their minds.

And so the whole notion goes down to doom on extended courtesies? The horrible Ping-Pong of manners? I don't think so. Such transactions are poetry, if we identify poetry with questions of how to live. And the reason it's so hard to say what they are can be inferred from Stevens's passage about waves and nobility.

When the Ghost appears in *Hamlet,* between lines 38 and 39 of the first scene, Marcellus thinks fast. Good executive material, he delegates responsibility well: "Thou art a scholar; speak to it, Horatio." Thirteen lines later when the Ghost is on its way offstage to Ghost-Piqua, Horatio commands it to stay, and it's gone.

I might have fluffed it, like Horatio. I'd rather not have fluffed it the way Marcellus ("a Danish officer," according to the *dramatis personae*) did: saving face in front of a ghost by putting his men on the spot. When Stevens makes one of his glimmery appearances in my mind, my best impulse is to say "Thanks."

(1980)

Horatian Hecht

"The true Horatian note is serenity," one of Horace's recent translators claims. Working backward from this reading of the work to the imagined life produces a familiar sketch:

> In 23 B.C., when he published the first three books of his lyrics, Horace was 42 years old, sure of his poetic gifts, secure in the favor of his emperor, Augustus, and living in ease and comfort on his Sabine Farm. . . . A worldly, high-spirited, cultivated man, Horace responds in his poetry to the myriad elements of Roman life he knew so well.

Horace himself contributed mightily to this. "Go little book," he urges,

> say I was born in poverty of a father once a slave
> but stretched my wings far beyond that humble nest:
> what you subtract from my descent, add to my virtues;
> say that I pleased the greatest Romans, in war and peace;
> say I was small, and early grey, and loved hot sunshine,
> swift to anger and yet easy to pacify. . . .
> (*Epistles* 1. 20, trans. Highet)

According to Suetonius's *Vita Horatii*, Augustus used to call Horace, teasingly, a "chaste little dick" and "charming little fellow." After reading some of the *sermones*, Augustus complained that he wasn't mentioned in them. "Can you be afraid that your reputation will suffer in later times because you appear to be my friend?" Thus when Horace shortly afterward published a new and thin book of poems that included some pieces specifically commissioned by Augustus, Augustus sent him a letter.

> Onysius has brought me your little book, which I accept in good part, small as it is, as making your excuses. But you seem to fear that your books will be bigger than you are yourself, though it is height you lack, not bulk. You are therefore permitted to write on a pint pot, so that your volume may be pot-bellied like yourself.

But what has this placid, modest, and chatty character to do with the author of the cruel and pessimistic *Epodes* or the melancholy sensualist ("chaste little dick," indeed) of the *Odes*?

In fact, what we conventionally value Horace for is least convincing in the poems. How threadbare his off-the-rack Epicureanism is, how dilatory the patriotism of the Roman odes, how donnish the *Ars Poetica* (Epistles 2.3). Horace's great and elusive subject is happiness, and in poetry, as in life, happiness can't be described so well as it can be embodied.

When Horace pictures Pindar as "the Theban swan" and himself as being

> just like a small bee
> sipping each sweet blossom of thyme and roving
> through the thick groves, over the slopes of Tiber
> rich with streams—so, cell upon cell, I labor
> moulding my poems . . .
> *(Odes* 4. 2, trans. Highet)

he is generally thought to be exercising a charming modesty as well as comparing the stature of Greek to Latin poetry, but he is also describing the difference between a poet with a solid religious context and subject matter (Pindar), and a poet like himself, the diligent attendant of the ineffable. With what sadness he must have written, in his *Ars Poetica, non satis est pulchra esse poemata* (it's not enough for poems to be beautiful). C. H. Sisson has wisely suggested that the most comparable modern text to the *Ars Poetica* is Pound's "A Stray Document," in *Make It New*. Pound, too, despaired because he could only make his poems beautiful, and when he tried to stuff them with truths, they didn't cohere.

In his last years James Wright spoke frequently of his devotion to Horace, and, in an interview, referring to the first thirteen lines of the *Ars Poetica,* of

> the ideal, what elsewhere I've called the Horatian ideal, the attempt finally to write a poem that will be put together so carefully that it does produce a single unifying effect. I still conceive of a poem as being a thing which one can make rather than as a matter of direct expression . . .

i.e., a way to embody what can't be said directly.

Such an understanding of the poetic enterprise is naturally haunted by the question of whether the unspeakable is truly unspeakable or merely a measurement of where a particular poet's courage and skill run out. This situation is like a lifetime of unanswered missives to the beloved, and thus a Horatian temperament is often drawn to the theme of art as a consolation, or at least as a steadying and leveling force, as lithium is for manic-depressives. Perhaps the melancholy to which the Horatian temperament is so susceptible is equivalent to the manic-depressive's suspicion that the loss of extreme highs and lows is also a loss of vivacity and authenticity.

Anthony Hecht muses as steadily on such matters as any of our poets. A characteristic poem, "The Cost," begins *Millions of Strange Shadows* (1977).

> Instinct with joy, a young Italian banks
> Smoothly around the base
> Of Trajan's column. . . .

The young man is on a Vespa, "at one with him in a centaur's race." Hecht wants to allude here both to chariot races and to *Lear*. "But to the girdle do the gods inherit, / Beneath is all the fiend's." The young man's girlfriend is riding with him. The obduracy of lust and the rhyme of *lust* and *dust* are recurrent tropes in Hecht. The Vespa is circling Trajan's column, erected to celebrate the successful prosecution of the Dacian Wars.

> And even Trajan, of his imperial peers
>   Accounted "the most just,"
>
> Honored by Dante, by Gregory the Great
>   Saved from Eternal Hell,
> Swirls in the motes kicked up by the cough and spate
>   Of the Vespa's blue exhaust,
> And a voice whispers inwardly, "My soul,
>   it is the cost, the cost,"
>
> Like some unhinged Othello, who's just found out
>   That justice is no more,
> While Cassio, Desdemona, Iago shout
>   Like true Venetians all,
> "Go screw yourself; all's fair in love and war!"
>   And the bright standards fall.
>
> Better they should not hear that whispered phrase,
>   The young Italian couple.
> Surely the mind in all its brave assays
>   Must put much thinking by,
> To be, as Yeats would have it, free and supple
>   As a long-legged fly.
>
> Look at their slender purchase, how they list
>   Like a blown clipper, brought
> To the lively edge of peril, to the kissed
>   Lip, the victor's crown,
> The prize of life. Yet one unbodied thought
>   Could topple them, bring down
>
> The whole shebang. And why should they take thought
>   Of all that ancient pain,
> The Danube winters, the nameless young who fought,
>   The blood's uncertain lease?
> Or remember that that fifteen-year campaign
>   Won seven years of peace?

The allusive machinery of the poem is considerable. In parts of the poem I have not quoted he mentions Calder's

mobiles and, alluding to *Lear* again, "samphire-tufted cliffs
which, though unseen, / Are known." The effect is to marshal
against the erosive costs of living the achieved poise of the
arts, and the implicit result is the Pyrrhic ratio of fifteen to
seven on which the poem ends.

Hecht's virtuosity was apparent from the beginning. *A
Summoning of Stones* (1954), with its Orphic title, opens with a
double sonnet and demonstrates a canny mastery of the pe-
riod style—a poetry of sobered wit rooted in the metaphysi-
cal poets, allusive, sceptical, urbane. Given to religious, myth-
ological, and historical occasions, these poems owe more,
perhaps, to Allen Tate than to any of the other elder poets
by whom Hecht might have been influenced. The intellec-
tual tone is a warily resigned humanism; we see in these
poems how much Hecht's generation grew up in the mag-
netic influence of Arnold's *Culture and Anarchy* and Eliot's
essays. Of course Hecht was later to send up Arnold in his
famous parody, "The Dover Bitch." And a close reading of *A
Summoning of Stones* reveals a skepticism about what art can
and cannot do that is at least partially at war with the
tension-resolving period style Hecht was not so much work-
ing in as working his way through.

"A Poem for Julia," "The Gardens of the Villa d'Este," "A
Roman Holiday," and "Alceste in the Wilderness" all bulge
interestingly from their battles between an elegant style and a
distrust of elegant art. In "Japan" the speaker tells how he
thought of Japan as a child, during World War II and after-
ward. Here's the second of the poem's seven stanzas:

> A child's quick sense of the ingenious stamped
> All their invention: toys I used to get
> At Christmastime, or the peculiar, cramped
> > Look of their alphabet.
> > Fragile and easily destroyed,
> > Those little boats of celluloid
> Driven by camphor round the bathroom sink,
> And delicate the folded paper prize
> > Which, dropped into a drink
> Of water, grew up right before your eyes.

In the poem the speaker, too, grows up right before your eyes. Here's the last stanza:

> Now the quaint early image of Japan
> That was so charming to me as a child
> Seems like a bright design upon a fan,
> Of water rushing wild
> On rocks that can be folded up,
> A river which the wrist can stop
> With a neat flip, revealing merely sticks
> And silk of what had been a fan before,
> And like such winning tricks,
> It shall be buried in excelsior.

In the long interval between *A Summoning of Stones* and *The Hard Hours* (1967), Hecht's style shifted significantly. In the words of Ted Hughes,

> He did the most difficult thing of all: this most fastidious and elegant of poets shed every artifice and began to write with absolute raw simplicity and directness.

I offer Hughes's words not because I concur wholly with them, but because they measure the surprise with which fellow poets met Hecht's long-awaited book.

Certainly Hecht's justly famous poem "A Hill," the first in *The Hard Hours*, signals a new tone in its opening lines.

> In Italy, where this sort of thing can occur,
> I had a vision once—though you understand
> It was nothing at all like Dante's, or the visions of saints,
> And perhaps not a vision at all. I was with some friends,
> Picking my way through a warm sunlit piazza
> In the early morning. A clear fretwork of shadows
> From huge umbrellas littered the pavement and made
> A sort of lucent shallows in which was moored
> A small navy of carts.

The elegance here is agreeably offhanded, and the passage allows Hecht to indulge to good effect his love of describing effects of light and shadow, of the effervescent.

Books, coins, old maps,
Cheap landscapes and ugly religious prints
Were all on sale. The colors and noise
Like the flying hands were gestures of exultation,
So that even the bargaining
Rose to the ear like a voluble godliness.
And then, when it happened, the noises suddenly stopped,
And it got darker; pushcarts and people dissolved
And even the great Farnese Palace itself
Was gone, for all its marble; in its place
Was a hill, mole-colored and bare. It was very cold,
Close to freezing, with a promise of snow.
The trees were like old ironwork gathered for scrap
Outside a factory wall. There was no wind,
And the only sound for a while was the little click
Of ice as it broke in the mud under my feet.
I saw a piece of ribbon snagged on a hedge,
But no other sign of life. And then I heard
What seemed the crack of a rifle. A hunter, I guessed;
At least I was not alone. But just after that
Came the soft and papery crash
Of a great branch somewhere unseen falling to earth.

In contrast to the elaborately turned, recurring stanza forms of *The Hard Hours*, "A Hill" pauses here for its first stanza break.

And that was all, except for the cold and silence
That promised to last forever, like the hill.

Another stanza break.

Then prices came through, and fingers, and I was restored
To the sunlight and my friends. But for more than a week
I was scared by the plain bitterness of what I had seen.
All this happened about ten years ago,
And it hasn't troubled me since, but at last, today,
I remembered that hill; it lies just to the left
Of the road north of Poughkeepsie; and as a boy
I stood before it for hours in wintertime.

Not the vain splendor of the Farnese Palace but the gesticulating fingers of vendors and the crying of prices bring the speaker back to daily life with its costs and pools of shadows. There is a palpable though not literal suggestion of his own fingers returning from frostbite at the start of the third stanza, and the plain bitterness of his vision is not something in the landscape, but something he sees in himself by means of the landscape.

Elsewhere in *The Hard Hours*, in poems like "Third Avenue in Sunlight" and "The End of the Weekend," when the surface of things is peeled away or sundered, something that seems partly an implacable evil and partly a madness is revealed. "Lizards and Snakes" tells of two boys, related to the youngster recalled in "Japan," who torment an aunt with the lizards and snakes she hates and they are fascinated by. The poem is in three stanzas; I quote the last two.

> Aunt Martha had an unfair prejudice
>   Against them (as well as being cold
> Toward bats.) She was pretty inflexible in this,
>   Being a spinster and all, and old.
> So we used to slip them into her knitting box.
>   In the evening she'd bring in things to mend.
> And a nice surprise would slide out from under the socks.
> It broadened her life, as Joe said. Joe was my friend.
>
> But we never did it again after the day
>   Of the big wind when you could hear the trees
> Creak like rockingchairs. She was looking away
>   Off, and kept saying, "Sweet Jesus, please
> Don't let him near me. He's as like as twins.
>   He can crack us like lice with his fingernail.
> I can see him plain as a pikestaff. Look how he grins
> And swinges the scaly horror of his folded tail."

Whatever the comparatively plain style Hecht perfected for *The Hard Hours* refers to in his experience is of course his business and not ours, but in the poems it seems to embody an unadorned peril from which the blandishments of art cannot so much restore us as distract us.

Two poems poised against each other in *Millions of Strange*

Shadows suggest a conflict that recapitulates the terms of Hecht's first two books. The first poem is "Dichtung und Wahrheit," and is dedicated by Cyrus Hoy, a colleague of Hecht's when he was teaching at the University of Rochester. The poem asks the old question: what does the study of humane letters mean? The diction and supple turns of the first stanza remind us of *A Summoning of Stones*, though of course "Dichtung und Wahrheit" is in Hecht's mature and not apprentice style.

> The Discus Thrower's marble heave,
>   Captured in mid-career,
> That polished poise, that Parian arm
>   Sleeved only in the air,
> Vesalian musculature, white
>   As the mid-winter moon—
> This, and the clumsy snapshot of
>   An infantry platoon,
> Those grubby and indifferent men,
>   Lounging in bivouac,
> Their rifles aimless in their laps,
>   Stop history in its tracks.

How can we invent a continuity of feeling with the past? Perhaps a certain linguistic sophistication helps, in which we might speak the dialects of different historical moments, so far as we are able. To know the names of the classical sculptors is a beginning, and to be able to reach without strain for the apt pun of "aimless. . . ."

The second half of the poem (I've quoted one of three stanzas in the first half) begins by assertion:

> We begin with the supreme donnée, the world,
> Upon which every text is commentary,
> And yet they play each other . . .

and the poem concludes,

> We begin with the supreme donnée, the word.

The very next poem is "A Voice at a Seance."

It is rather strange to be speaking, but I know you are there
Wanting to know, as if it were worth knowing.
Nor is it important that I died in combat
In a good cause or an indifferent one.
Such things, it may surprise you, are not regarded.
Something too much of this.

You are bound to be disappointed,
Wanting to know, are there any trees?
It is all different from what you suppose,
And the darkness is not darkness exactly,
But patience, silence, withdrawal, the sad knowledge
That it was almost impossible not to hurt anyone
Whether by action or inaction.
At the beginning of course there was a sense of loss,
Not of one's own life, but of what seemed
The easy, desirable lives one might have led.
Fame or wealth are hard to achieve,
And goodness even harder;
But the cost of them all is a familiar deformity
Such as everyone suffers from:
An allergy to certain foods, nausea at the sight of blood,
A fear of heights or claustrophobia.
What you learn has nothing to do with joy,
Nor with sadness, either. You are mostly silent.
You come to a gentle indifference about being thought
Either a fool or someone with valuable secrets.
It may be that the ultimate wisdom
Lies in saying nothing.
I think I may already have said too much.

The identification of the speaker as a soldier and the use of the adjective "indifferent," also used in the first stanza of "Dichtung und Wahrheit," gives us the eerie sense that the speaker of this poem might be one of the soldiers in the photograph from the preceding poem. In this poem, of course, we have no gift, no donnée, but cost. The poem adopts an old trick of science fiction; it purports to describe a future but seems, unsettlingly enough, to describe a queasily familiar present. Perhaps we could perceive it without seance if it weren't for the beautiful distractions of art, like a procession of gorgeously confected clouds. Behind them, if we could but see, there might well be a hill, "mole-colored and bare." Of course there are no trees, for this is *paysage démoralisé*.

One of the epigraphs to *The Venetian Vespers* (1979) is from *Moby-Dick:* "Though in many of its aspects this visible world seems formed in love, the invisible spheres were formed in fright." These frights are not only lizards and snakes, but far too much of our recent history. "Apprehensions" in *Millions of Strange Shadows* and "An Overview" in *The Venetian Vespers* eloquently embody, respectively, the haunting presences of the Holocaust and the Vietnam War.

The Horatian temperament has always poised against organized terrors as well as more private ones the virtues of personal civilization—work well done, love pursued as a benign sport, the good report of one's peers, and so on. So for Hecht to include in *The Venetian Vespers* two versions "freely adapted from Horace," as he identifies them, is quite germane to his ongoing meditation on the powers and impotences of art.

The two poems Hecht adapts are both widely known—*Odes* 1.1 and *Odes* 1.5.

Horace's first ode is addressed to Maecenas, his patron, whose interest in Horace's talents led to the Sabine Farm and a sinecure. Since Maecenas was also an intimate of Augustus, his patronage meant as secure a social position as volatile Rome could offer a poet, and a lifetime to write. Such largesse required a stupendous thank-you letter, and Horace set jauntily to work.

> Maecenas, descended from olden kings,
> my rampart and sweet admiration. . . .

The poem goes on to list the various ways men seek their happiness: some race chariots, some strive in politics, some farm, some seek leisure and some battle. But he just wishes a little honor for his verses, and, indeed, if Maecenas would bestow his approval on Horace, Horace would think himself singled out by Euterpe himself.

> and should you list me among the lyric bards
> I should nudge the stars with my lifted head.

The nudged stars may well be a joke about Horace's height. There's a loose, banter-among-old-friends tone to Horace's original that's part of its relaxed, beguiling sophistication. After all, the favor the poem seems to be asking has in fact in large measure already been granted, and so whatever element of submission there might be in application to Maecenas has already gone by the boards.

Here's Hecht's version, called "Application for a Grant."

> Noble executors of the munificent testament
> Of the late John Simon Guggenheim, distinguished bunch
> Of benefactors, there are certain kinds of men
> Who set their hearts on being bartenders,
> For whom a life upon duck-boards, among fifths,
> Tapped kegs and lemon twists, crowded with lushes
> Who can master neither their bladders nor consonants,
> Is the only life, greatly to be desired.
> There's the man who yearns for the White House, there to compose
> Rhythmical lists of enemies, while someone else
> Wants to be known to the *Tour d'Argent's* headwaiter.
> As the Sibyl of Cumae said: It takes all kinds.
> Nothing could bribe your Timon, your charter member
> Of the Fraternal Order of Grizzly Bears to love
> His fellow, whereas it's just the opposite
> With interior decorators; that's what makes horse races.
> One man may have a sharp nose for tax shelters,
> Screwing the IRS with mirth and profit;
> Another devotes himself to his shell collection,
> Deaf to his offspring, indifferent to the feats
> With which his wife hopes to attract his notice.
> Some at the Health Club sweating under bar bells
> Labor away like grunting troglodytes,
> Smelly and thick and inarticulate,
> Their brains squeezed out through their pores by sheer
>   exertion.
> As for me, the prize for poets, the simple gift
> For amphybrachs strewn by a kind Euterpe,
> With perhaps a laurel crown of the evergreen
> Imperishable of your fine endowment
> Would supply my modest wants, who dream of nothing
> But a pad on Eighth Street and your approbation.

This is a curious performance. The ostensible objects of satire here—drunks, Nixon, the muscle-bound pinheads at the Health Club—are fish in a barrel. The jibe about the Fraternal Order of Grizzly Bears smells as much of snobbery as the jibe about interior decorators does of homophobia. The level of wit is, for Hecht, unusually low; there's a rather ponderous money-does-too-grow-on-trees joke ("evergreen / imperishable of your fine endowment") but mostly the tone is not only sour but curdled. The "pad on Eighth Street" is, I take it, a stock property of the feckless bohemian's fantasy life, though Auden had a place there.

The reader can hear the engines of satire churning in this poem, but against whom is the satire directed? Surely not at all those easy targets, so it must be directed at the speaker.

Whereas in Horace's original the fiction is that the speaker and poet are the same, the opposite is surely true here. For one thing (here's a parallel with the original) Hecht already had his Guggenheim. And for another, by including his version of Horace in his own book, Hecht chose to further complicate the relationship of poet to speaker by adding translator to the cast of characters.

Well, then, whom does the speaker represent? Poets who like to feel superior to the middle class but who in doing so betray a sensibility hopelessly middle class? That kind of satire uses one end of a snake to beat the other end to death. Bad poets? The proposition that all urge for recognition and ease in a life in the arts is fundamentally crass? Or is this the "plain bitterness" of "The Hill" projected on the blank screen of the world?

Hecht does far better with *Odes* 1.5. Horace's original begins (as in the case of 1.1; I'm using W. G. Shepherd's translation):

> What slender youth besprinkled with fragrant oils
> now crowds you, Pyrrha, amid the roses
> in some convenient grotto?
> For whom do you dress that yellow hair . . . [?]

And the three remaining quatrains anticipate that Pyrrha's imagined current lover will, as the speaker once did, compare his time with Pyrrha to a close call at sea. There's an allusive metaphor at the end of the poem that's hard to translate without, in effect, building a footnote into the translation, for it refers to the custom of hanging on a certain votive plaque to Neptune the damp clothes in which one escaped death at sea. Here's Hecht's version, called "An Old Malediction."

> What well-heeled knuckle-head, straight from the unisex
> Hairstylist and bathed in *Russian Leather,*
> Dallies with you these summer days, Pyrrha,
> In your expensive sublet? For whom do you
> Slip into something simple by, say, Gucci?
> The more fool he who has mapped out for himself
> The saline latitudes of incontinent grief.
> Dazzled though he be, poor dope, by the golden looks
> Your locks fetched up out of a bottle of *Clairol,*
> He will know that the wind changes, the smooth sailing
> Is done for, when the breakers wallop him broadside,
> When he's rudderless, dismasted, thoroughly swamped
> In that mindless rip-tide that got the best of me,
> Once, when I ventured on your deeps, Piranha.

Hecht has left Neptune's plaque out of his version and made other metaphorical use ("dismasted") of the storm. And since Hecht's version argues throughout the likelihood that Pyrrha is a shallow creature, the torque he puts on "deeps" in the last line is sly.

The metamorphosis of "Pyrrha" to "Piranha" glosses an element added to Horace by Hecht, rather than freely adapted: bitterness. Except for "Clairol" and "Piranha" most of it is in the first five lines; one can perhaps feel the distasteful shudder strongest at "Russian Leather." It is all too easy, as it was almost throughout "An Application for a Grant." The convulsive brilliance of a line like "the saline latitudes of incontinent grief" may have been an attempt to wrench the translator away from his loathing so that he could, as he did, perform a splendid job with what's left of Horace's poem.

As we have seen, the virtuoso style of Hecht's earliest poems has matured along with this remarkable poet. It is in eclipse for whole poems at a time in *The Hard Hours* and later books, while the poet gives his abilities over to embodying some brute and bare thing from which the lucent polish of a more embellished art might reflect and deflect our gaze. In his best poems the two styles and the two attitudes of mind they embody contest to achieve a balance—I'm thinking of the Vespa-riding Italian youth in "The Cost" as one of Hecht's central figures for this balance—between, at one extreme, a merely pyrotechnic art, and, at the other, an obdurate thing so powerful that it beggars not only art but the will to speak at all ("I think I may already have said too much.").

Of course one job of a poet is not to fall silent.

Hecht's formidable descriptive powers are at their happiest and best when working on the effervescent, "the splendor of the insubstantial." This love of what is ever-changing outside the self makes particularly poignant sense for a poet to whom the mysteries of the self, and thus the mysteries of the species in microcosm, can perhaps be figured by a bare, mole-colored hill.

And one senses in his best writing how little accommodation he has made with the conflict as well as how masterfully he has learned to embody that dilemma. I'll close this essay by quoting the concluding passage of "The Venetian Vespers." The speaker of the poem, who is of course not Hecht himself, is looking at the Venetian sky from a window.

> Against a diorama of palest blue
> Cloud-curds, cloud-stacks, cloud-bushes sun themselves.
> Giant confections, impossible meringues,
> Soft coral reefs and powdery tumuli
> Pass in august processions and calm herds.
> Great stadiums, grandstands and amphitheaters,
> The tufted, opulent litters of the gods
> They seem; or laundered bunting, well-dressed wigs,
> Harvests of milk-white, Chinese peonies
> That visibly rebuke our stinginess.
> For all their ghostly presences, they take on
> A colorful nobility at evening.
> Off to the east the sky begins to turn
> Lilac so pale it seems a mood of gray,
> Gradually, like the death of virtuous men.

Streaks of electrum richly underline
The slow, flat-bottomed hulls, those floated lobes
Between which quills and spokes of light fan out
Into carnelian reds and nectarines,
Nearing a citron brilliance at the center,
The searing furnace of the glory hole
That fires and fuses clouds of muscatel
With pencilings of gold. I look and look,
As though I could be saved simply by looking—
I, who have never earned my way, who am
No better than a viral parasite,
Or the lees of the Venetian underworld,
Foolish and muddled in my later years,
Who was never even at one time a wise child.

(1989)

Moving Around

In a recurring childhood dream I was separated from my
family. We'd be out walking and a crack would appear in the
earth, or a widening river. I imagined myself the dream's
unwilling victim. It was years before I understood that the
dream was as much about my urge to be separate as it was
about my fear of separation.

As I grew older the other characters changed. It would be
my wife and two sons together, me separate.

Though I didn't dream about them, other splits fit the pat-
tern. I would want to be both a part of and apart from some
community: a neighborhood, a team, a political movement
whose complaints I shared but whose rhetoric I hated. . . .

I used to have a morning paper route, played baseball and
basketball, had a dog named Spot. Troy, Ohio. When I was
about twelve my father left his job with the Soil Conservation
Service and went to work for a student exchange program,
Children's International Summer Villages.

Geography had seemed abstract to me, some pleasant puz-
zle. Now the vast world grew in my mind. My father wrote
letters to Finland, Japan. The family went to Europe. I began
to realize I was American, envied and disliked and judged for
that, and shaped by it. That fact went ahead of me somehow,
the way that being black might, or living in a shack by the river
and being three grades behind in school, poor Norbert.

We moved to Cincinnati, where CISV's American head-
quarters were. My father had been born there; so had I. We
had family there. I went back to Europe three times. I went to
boarding school in the Berkshire Hills, I went to college. Spot
was an aging snuffle. In Europe buildings sat on the same

spot for six hundred years—more, unless war broke them. They seemed more like stones than buildings I had known and the lives they passed through themselves seemed stable and claustrophobic.

I had lived in Ames, Iowa; Rosewood, Troy, and Cincinnati, Ohio; Sheffield, Massachusetts; New Haven, Connecticut. I was married and had a son. Moving meant opportunity. One left friends, but also dead ends, shames, bad times.

And landscape grew cumulative. A stream that ran through a roadside park near Rosewood flowed into a stream in the Berkshires. There were hollyhocks by the back steps in Troy, where I threw a tennis ball for hours against a strike zone I'd outlined on the shed door. When I got good at it, I'd load the bases, go 3-and-0, and then, nobody out, trying hard now, see if I could pitch my way out of the inning. One summer in New Haven I was doing odd jobs and worked for a family in Hamden. Beside the shed where they kept a huge glum goose at night, I found the hollyhocks unchanged, their dusty scent so thick it might as well not have rained for twelve years.

When I played those imaginary ball games, I sensed they wouldn't matter if I couldn't lose. But I could pitch an imaginary game in half an hour, and if I lost I'd pitch another, and another if I had to, until I'd won. I never slept with a loss. There'd be another game, I could be traded, there'd be another season, I could move.

I moved to North Carolina with my wife, then pregnant, and son. Two sons. Now my sport was basketball. I played on an otherwise all black team. Our mailman loved jazz and cognac, and so did I. I found out he had a team in a local league, and asked if I could play. It turned out to be the only integrated team in the league: blacks and whites played against but not with each other. I liked to pass; I liked to decide by where I'd pass if we'd run or set up plays; I liked to penetrate because it made the defense commit itself and the patterns shift. When we'd line up for the tip-off the guys on the other team, black or white, would say of one of my teammates, "I'll take number 6." Of me: "I'll take the white guy."

I've always loved in basketball its particular balance between pattern and improvisation. The rift is always there, but it shifts, and the play does, too, each moving the other. When I'm playing well I respond so well to this balance that I help cause it.

North Carolina was the first place I'd ever lived that I helped to cause a little how the place felt. A child is dwarfed by his parents, a student by his school. I was a graduate student in North Carolina, but I had two children, I knew as many people outside the university as in, I started a literary magazine with friends, I voted and paid taxes. We lived in an apartment complex. Toward the end I wanted to get away. I wrote a poem called "Moving" before we moved.

Moving

When we spurt off
in the invalid Volvo
flying its pennant of blue fumes,
the neighbors group and watch.
We twist away like a released balloon.

I'd written poems in high school, most of them about the sadness of adolescent life. I wrote a few in college, a dozen maybe, of which I finished four. Through the kindness of one of my professors, two were published. He didn't intervene in my poems' behalf, I'm sure; he only suggested I send them out and told me where I could use his name as one reason for asking the editor's attention. When I saw them in print I was proud, then scared. They were only technically good. Otherwise they were false. Worse than that, I had believed in them wholly when I wrote them, when I sent them off, when I first saw them in print. I could be false to myself, to the language I wrote in, in ways so subtle it took me weeks to notice and years to understand.

Like many adolescents, I had become a good liar. I lied about where I had been, about sex, about money, to my parents, teachers, friends, to myself. Such lies seem so crude, I thought I knew about them: I am saying X but the truth I am keeping to myself is Y.

The rift was in me. Such lies gave me power: I could *use* the language.

But, looking at my poems in print, I felt the force of something I didn't yet know about language: it is communal. Poets like to talk about the solitude of writing, but the language they use has passed through everyone who has ever spoken or read or written the same words, no matter how individually any poet combines those words. The lives of others are on the words, as palm oil is on coins long in circulation.

And there the poems were in print. I must have known my shame for those poems was as opaque to the few who read them as it was transparent to me. I didn't know enough about myself, about language, about the lives through which language passed on its way through me.

Teaching and writing poems brought me into a larger world. Landscape continued to be my deepest pleasure and most ambitious exploration. At Aurora, New York, the lake was four miles wide. In the spring Canada geese settled in for a month, foraging by day in the fields and flying back to the lake each dusk. In the winter the lake threw onto the shore, with its wave-smoothed rocks, gnarled chunks of ice. I could not—I who loved metaphor, transformation, change—make them into anything but themselves, and their resistance soothed me.

Aurora had six hundred residents and the college six hundred students. I liked the sparse population. The first full day we were there I walked with my sons to a cluster of houses down the road, where younger faculty with children lived. The kids all called it "the neighborhood." The boys looked around; everyone was indoors. "Where are the friends?" one of them asked. Soon they had friends.

I did, too. I wasn't lonely, but the rhythms of solitude and affection pulled me hard, surprised me.

The next year we moved to Ithaca and bought an old farmhouse on Krums Corners Road. Colonel Krum had run an inn, a stop on the stagecoach run north to Geneva, two hundred years ago. We had six apple trees, two pears, three cherries, blackberries, grapes, a hundred-yard-long stretch of multiflora roses on one side of the yard. Lilacs in three colors of bloom, peonies, and irises—my favorites. One cherry was an ornamental, beautiful for its three days of bloom in May.

My first book of poems had come out: now and then I'd be asked to give a reading somewhere. Every year when it came into bloom I was gone. I loved the place.

My wife and I began to fight, sometimes with long silences. In the midst of them I'd remember how the molecules in solid things, spoons or doors, are said to be constantly moving. Probably all our friends guessed before we did that we'd get divorced.

One day when I hadn't yet put up the screens on the second floor windows, I went out one window onto the roof over the front porch. The screens went on from the outside, so when I got them up I'd have sealed off my route back through the windows. She was to come prop the ladder against the porch so I could get down when I was done. But the phone rang, and she talked for a while. The boys were in the house, and my wife, and I was on the single side of the rift again. My terror was so pure I must have added to my childhood dream the still unconscious knowledge that I'd soon be divorced.

There were three huge sugar maples off the porch, forty or fifty feet tall. They interlaced at the top, and the boys and I played endlessly a game I invented called Rocket. I kicked a soccer ball high into the trees and as it fell it caromed off branches, trunks. Sometimes it fell four times as slowly for all its high pinball detours as it would by gravity. Sometimes it hit a thick branch on the way up and sliced back down. We tried different scoring systems: how much for a clean catch, how much for the first bounce, did two bounces count? The boys would giggle and make showboat catches, forgetting to sprawl until they had the ball snugly in. Or they would scuffle grimly, suddenly wanting to win by whatever rules we'd agreed on for the day, so intense I'd think they were holding their breaths except I could hear the rasps they breathed calming back down after flurries of effort or temper.

I wanted to climb down one of those maples, but the branches of all three fell just short of the porch roof. I was breathing like an old pump, hysterical, when my wife arrived with the ladder.

Some people like to tell about their lives, but that's not what I mean to do here. I'm interested in the biography of some images, some collisions between my emotional life and the language that binds me to others.

All that summer and the next year my dog, Underdog, killed woodchucks. He kept them out of the garden, though my neighbors' sheep drifted over one summer night, a cloud of teeth, and cropped the garden. They left the tomatoes and onions. We named Underdog after a character in a TV cartoon, a beagle with a cape who talked in couplets. Spot had been part beagle. Wally Cox was Underdog's voice. The boys watched Underdog every Saturday morning; often I watched with them.

I liked the traveling I did to give readings, or to work in poets-in-the-school programs. One spring I was working in schools in the Housatonic River Valley, where I'd been in boarding school years before. I was glad to be away from my eroding home, but I missed my wife and sons and felt guilty for being glad to be away. The lyrical gloom of adolescence came back to me as I was driving to Washington, Connecticut, along a road I remembered from bus trips made by the basketball team. In the motel where I stayed while I was working at Hotchkiss I wrote a poem with a deliberately lavish title:

Driving alongside the Housatonic River
Alone on a Rainy April Night

I remember asking
where does my shadow go at night?
I thought it went home,
it grew so sleek at dusk.
They said, you just don't
notice it, the way you don't tell yourself
how to walk or hear
a noise that doesn't stop.
But one wrong wobble
in the socket and inside the knee
chalk is falling, school
is over.
As if the ground were a rung
suddenly gone from a ladder,
the self, the shoulders bunched

against the road's each bump, the penis
with its stupid grin,
the whole rank slum of cells
collapses.
I feel the steering wheel
tug a little, testing.
For as long as that takes
the car is a sack of kittens
weighed down by stones.
The headlights chase a dark ripple
across some birch trunks.
I know it's there, water
hurrying over the shadow of water.

Soon my wife and I were separated, and I was separated
from my sons, too. As soon as we could agree on the terms we
would be divorced. We couldn't. Lawyers handled the last part.

I moved to Andover, Massachusetts, where I lived on an acre
in young woods (maples, birch, about twenty years old), and
taught in Boston. The boys lived an hour away. I moved to be
near them while divorce details were worked out. The divorce
went through. The county sheriff served the papers and con-
gratulated me. I did a lot of readings. I'd been to Louisiana and
walked over the rice plantation, now restored, where Audubon
made his first bird paintings. He shot the birds first. He was a
tutor to the owner's daughter and had his afternoons free. I'd
been to Tucson and kept driving out to the resistant desert, as
fiercely itself against my transforming imagination as the
mountains were in Colorado when I'd been there.

My job in Boston was for one year only; soon I'd move
again. The boys would live with me every summer, and could
visit during every school vacation I could afford to transport
them to wherever I would be. It began to look as if I'd be in
Colorado, and I liked that prospect. I'd met a woman I
wanted to live with: I revised some of the myths about solitude
I'd been telling myself so long.

I hadn't been in Europe for ten years. I went to England to
visit my parents, who lived there now, and took the boys. I
went to Canisy, in Normandy, when a plaque was put on the
house where the French poet Jean Follain was born. It would

have been his seventieth birthday, but he'd been killed by a car in the Place de la Concorde. I'd spent four years working, with a friend, on translations of Follain's prose poems. His widow, a tiny, tough, and generous woman, showed us St. Lô, razed in World War II when the Allies took Normandy. I was an "American" again. From the train from Paris I was moved by orchards that reminded me of the house I'd loved and sold in Ithaca. Dairy cattle moved among the apple trees; though I've never lived with them they made me weep. I realized I'd become an American without knowing it. The boy who went to foreign movies, to Europe, who in his teens read Ionesco as fast as Grove Press published him but delayed reading James's *The American Scene* until he was thirty (Mme. Ionesco came to Canisy for the Follain ceremony)—the same boy grown older had learned from travel and love of his sons and love of the American language to be American. Perhaps I learned it from failing, as banks or businesses or marriages are said to fail. One declares bankruptcy—a kind of confession—and moves on.

I would be going to Colorado early in the summer, and as soon as the boys were out of school in New Hampshire they'd come out.

In my early poems, like "Moving," time is like a lens opening and slicing shut. If I imagined something emblematic, in significant posture, I could get a good picture. The method was good for the bases loaded, 3-and-0, none out; the strain on the pitcher's face tells all.

But little of life organizes itself into symbolic moments. And symbolic moments may distort as much as they summarize; indeed, they may distort *by* summarizing.

There are after all the times when a pitcher has to live with having lost, as I would not allow myself to do when I was young, bending my private world as easily as water seems to bend light.

After learning to write poems like "Moving," I wanted to learn to write about different kinds of time. As in a snapshot, in "Moving" it is hard to tell what any of the people thinks about the event. This neutrality is an improvement from my early youth, when I would melodramatically fear the separation in my recurrent dream without realizing that I also wanted it.

Perhaps the adjective "released" suggests the speaker's attitude toward leaving his neighbors. I won't speak for the poem, but I remember the day I left. My wife and sons had gone ahead while I finished the heavy work of moving, cleaned our apartment out, haggled with the landlord for the return of our deposit money. It was nearly one hundred degrees. I was glad to be going back north, singing, waving my free arm in time, sweating so heavily in the thick heat I might as well have been under spot lights, though under them I could never have been so giddily oblivious to how I must have looked as motorists grumbled by in the sapping sunlight.

The poem about driving alongside the river pleased me when I wrote it. The man in the poem is in one place, at one time, but he carries his childhood with him, his schooling, his adolescence; no snapshot can do that. We see him alone—daydreaming would be the word, except in the poem it is night. He is with those central images and myths about his own life that impede and enliven him. Though as I read the poem it is not a difficult choice, he chooses, when for an instant the possibility of not continuing seems sharp and not silly, to keep moving.

I am not surprised to find him in a poem called "Moving Again." I speak of him as "him" because he is not me. He clearly shares certain crucial situations with me (his sons have the same names as mine); he resembles me more than anyone else I know or imagine. But when I am done with a poem I walk away from it; he stays in it. In many of my poems he does not appear, or appears disguised as others.

Perhaps I have invented a sophisticated version of those imaginary playmates children have. My son Sebastian had one for a while. Sebastian's friend pulled off, at the end of his life, several amazing feats, and adults were getting skeptical about him; so Sebastian announced one day he was dead. "How did it happen?" "He got run over on his way to the store to get cheese for his family." Since his family had never been mentioned before, it was clear they were us, who had been laughing at this now dead hero, his last heroism a small generosity for us.

That's the way I like to see these imaginary selves go. They should be left behind, in some poem, on some imaginary street, whenever the continuing and moving self no longer needs them. Our poetry is full of them—Kees's Robinson, Berryman's Henry, almost everyone's "I." They are in postures of revealing, insupportable loss, held in house arrest by the beautiful poems they live in. The poet keeps moving; and, when I am the poet, keeps writing about it, wanting to include more.

When I got to Colorado I wrote the poem called "Moving Again." Nicky is the son of friends here who used to live in Illinois. I had a high-school girlfriend named Verna. And in some high-school anthology there was a story about people transported (though the story suggests the vehicle may have been only their yearning to be moved) to a magical planet named Verna. They gathered in a barn, sat on benches, and were taken away, or so I remember the story. There was some reason, like the impending end of this planet, why they wanted to be gone. But the story wasn't good enough to resist my imagination, to impose its truth on mine. So I don't remember the story's reason.

Moving Again

At night the mountains look like dim
hens. In a few geological eras
new mountains may
shatter the earth's shell
and poke up like stone wings.
Each part must serve for a whole.
I bring my sons to the base
of the foothills and we go up.
From a scruff of Ponderosa
pines we startle gaudy swerves
of magpies who settle in our rising
wake. Then there's a blooming
prickly pear. "Jesus, Dad, what's that?"
Willy asks. It's like a yellow tulip
grafted to a cactus: it's a beautiful
wound the cactus puts out

to bear fruit and be healed.
If I lived with my sons
all year I'd be less sentimental
about them. We go up
to the mesa top and look down
at our new home town. The thin air
warps in the melting light
like the aura before a migraine.
The boys are tired. A tiny magpie
fluffs into a pine far below
and further down in the valley
of child support and lights
people are opening drawers.
One of them finds a yellowing
patch of newsprint with a phone
number pencilled on it
from Illinois, from before they moved, before
Nicky was born. Memory
is our root system.
"Verna," he says to himself
because his wife's in another room,
"whose number do you suppose this is?"

(1976)

On the Tennis Court at Night

"What is it about tennis that appeals to you?" Galway Kinnell was asked by an interviewer in 1975, and here's how he answered.

> If you really concentrate in tennis, mind, body, spirit, all become one thing—in this it's like poetry—a tremendously happy activity. But it's also the opposite of poetry, because it's an entirely escapist activity. I like it for both reasons. When the world is too much with you, you just put on your white vanishing-clothes and enter that court laid out in pure, Euclidean lines—and live for a few hours with increased life, like a wild animal.

Kinnell goes on to name other poets obsessed by tennis: Pound, Hart Crane, Berryman, Roethke (who coached the game as well as played it), and Jarrell.

In a letter written in 1950, Jarrell wrote similarly of how the game can simultaneously lift you out of yourself and remind you of your inescapable home in yourself.

> I played a lot of tennis this summer; I won a singles tournament at Cape Cod in a very long match, the most satisfying I ever played. When one does what one *should*, beyond one's expectations, it's a queer feeling—one gets as much used to one's faults as to the world's, and yet they are an obsessive grief in a way the world's never are.

I can't prove it, but I think the pun of "fault" in Jarrell's letter was probably unconscious. Intentionally made, it would have been lost on his correspondent, whose English was very good but nonetheless a second language, and who was neither an avid tennis player nor the compulsive punster Jarrell was. In any case the passage implies a double purpose, for Jarrell, in playing tennis.

On the one hand, the game is humbling: it teaches you over and over your faults and that you should, more or less, come to terms with those faults. But on the other hand, when and in fact because you do more or less come to terms with those faults, there are times when you play so well and so fluidly that you seem to transcend them, to be, more or less, faultless.

Kinnell's vocabulary is different, but he also invokes in tennis a dual power. On the one hand you are made whole and wholly mortal by the game: mind, body, and spirit converge. But on the other hand you escape into an increased life and are like a wild animal. Notice that the escape is from a "world . . . too much with you," so that you play "out of this world." Current tennis slang has it that you play "in the zone," or, as Martina Navratilova told Bud Collins in a Wimbledon interview, "I really zoned in the third set."

The truth is that you would not want to be long out of this world, for that is quite literally to be dead. But to see only "this humanized, familiar world as if it were all there is," as Kinnell has it in another interview, is a kind of willed blindness. I think Kinnell speaks of tennis the way he does in the passage I quote above because the dual power he finds in tennis rhymes with a dual power in poetry, particularly in Kinnell's own poetry. Kinnell's poems relish and love to describe the physical world, and exult in the kind of loving attention to physical life that makes mind, body, and spirit all become one thing; his poems have great powers of concentration. But at the same time his poems love to peer *through* the physical world toward the vast cosmos in which our world is as but a cinder.

"On the Tennis Court at Night," from *Mortal Acts, Mortal Words* (1980), is a characteristic meditation on these dual impulses in Kinnell's work. Here are the first eleven of the poem's fifty-one lines.

We step out on the green rectangle
in moonlight; the lines glow,
which for many have been the only lines
of justice. We remember
the thousand trajectories the air has erased
of that close-contested last set—
blur of volleys, soft arcs of drop shots,
huge ingrown loops of lobs with topspin
which went running away, crosscourts recrossing
down to each sweet (and in exact proportion, bitter)
❂ in Talbert and Olds' *The Game of Doubles in Tennis*.

The lines glow because of the moonlight, but also, meta-
phorically, because they *can* represent, when so little else can,
an idea of justice. They're allied to ❂ marks in what most
experts—I am not one and so am relying on their testimony—
think the best book on doubles strategy; these marks represent
the ideal shot placement in various given situations likely to
arise in orderly play. The ❂ marks, the lines, and indeed the
idea of orderly play—as opposed to an improvised play in
which accumulated wisdoms about the size of the court, the
positioning of the players, and the most advantageous shots to
play in given situations are ignored—represent a communal
and historical achievement of the "humanized, familiar
world," and also represent a grid of expected and usually prof-
itable procedure against which brilliant improvisations can be
measured. Without the grid certain inspired shots might seem
merely random.

The actual play of the last set is lost to memory, and per-
haps it is just as well. It would resemble one of those time-
lapse photographs of night traffic along a highway, or the
surface of much-skated ice. And the more the trajectories
obscured our view of the pure, Euclidean lines of the court
the less the trajectories would have any reason for being.

Here's an excerpt from a 1971 interview:

NYQ: In our *New York Quarterly* craft interviews we have tried
to be as objective as possible and not to get too involved with
feelings and emotions about things, but stay with craft and
style.

Kinnell: Matters I don't know anything about.

And here's an excerpt from a 1976 interview:

Interviewer: I know you've said that you distrust discussions of poetry that are technical—

Kinnell: I *think* I distrust them. Perhaps I like them without knowing it.

It's easy to see what's going on in the *New York Quarterly* interview. I can hardly imagine a poet who would find the question—which isn't a question, but a self-congratulation—more obnoxious. Surely Kinnell doesn't mean that he knows nothing about craft and style, but that to talk about what he knows without reference to feelings and emotions about things seems to him nonsense. And I think we can see what's going on in the 1976 interview. He means that he's wary of the terms in which such discussions are often conducted, but that if they did not perforce chop into pieces what the poet struggles to make whole, he'd damn well be interested in the topic.

The circumstance where a poet can write what he best knows about such matters is in writing a poem, and "On the Tennis Court at Night" does so, metaphorically. Metaphor does not discuss "one thing in terms of another," as we may have been wrongly told at some point in our schooling, but discusses several things all in terms of each other. Usually, of course, a poem has an ostensible central topic—in this case, tennis.

Also, a poem can become itself a kind of large metaphor for the capacity of intelligent feeling to resolve what seems paradoxical when it is argued in prose. How can a highly formal and conventional game like doubles release one to feeling like a wild animal? And how can one by extreme concentration on immediate physical life seem to belong both to it and to the larger and essentially inhuman life of the cosmos?

In the "Author's Note" to *The Avenue Bearing the Initial of*

Christ into the New World: Poems 1946–64 (though the book was published in 1974, the note is dated 1970), Kinnell wrote:

> I have chosen these poems out of some hundreds I wrote—and mercilessly revised—in my late teens and early twenties.
>
> It might have turned out better for me if, during that period of my life, I had written less and given myself more to silence and waiting. At least those arduous searches for the right iambic beat and the rhyme word seem now like time which could have been better spent. I will never know, and in any event, it is not possible for me to regret a travail which released in me so much energy and excitement, to which I gave myself so entirely, and which saved me. The leftovers, these few pieces of verse, whatever their worth for someone else, I hold in kindly affection.
>
> As I was preparing this collection, Charles G. Bell produced from his files all the first, unrevised versions of my poems—versions which I myself had long since thrown away. I discovered those first versions were almost always superior to the revised ones—which says little for my powers of recognition and revision. The poems in this book, therefore, are mostly in their earlier form, some of them cut considerably, others patched up here and there with lines from the revisions.

It's a good thing, we speculated earlier, that the trajectories of all those volleys, drop shots, lobs, and cross-courts are erased, and doubly so, for there are two trajectories for every shot in tennis, at least the way I play tennis. There's the imaginary trajectory leading from the racket to the ❂ mark exactly where Talbert and Olds would have me hit the shot, and then there's the trajectory of the shot I actually hit.

Kinnell is describing something similar in his "Author's Note," with "the right iambic beat and the rhyme word" standing for the same purpose as the ❂ mark in Talbert and Olds.

But of course the poem is not made by discovering the right iambic beat or rhyme word, but rather from the tension between some such imaginary ideal and what the poet actually finds for himself to say. The function of forms and conventions may be to enable that tension. In tennis it is that tension against which, even more than against opponents, I play. And in writing it is a similar tension—I think of it as being like an electrical resistance—that a poet hopes will blunt what is merely habitual and facile in what he discovers to say.

> The breeze has carried them off but we still hear
> the mutters, the doublefaulter's groans,
> cries of "Deuce!" or "Love Two!",
> squeak of tennis shoes, grunt of overreaching,
> all dozen extant tennis quips—"Just out!"
> or, "About right for you?" or, "Want to change partners?"
> and *baaah* of sheep translated very occasionally
> into *thonk* of well-hit ball, among the pure
> right angles and unhesitating lines
> of this arena where every man grows old
> pursuing that repertoire of perfect shots.

"The breeze has carried them off," this passage begins, and "them" refers to the trajectories of all the shots of the last set, but another breeze like it will carry off the mutters, groans, squeaks, grunts, and quips that Kinnell enumerates, and eventual breezes will carry off the players themselves. It might be closer to the spirit of the poem to think of the players as not carried off, when that day comes, but translated, the way sheep gut gets translated to racket strings.

Here's Kinnell speaking in an interview:

> Yes, as death has two aspects—the extinction, which we fear, and the flowing away into the universe, which we desire—there is a conflict within us that I want to deal with.

The lines quoted above are characteristic in their loving litany of physical detail and especially characteristic in the way that litany builds along with its own rhetorical momentum a kind of shadow momentum, an accumulating fatigue and sense of the gravity of physical life, so that the prospect of release, of flowing away into the universe, mollifies the more terrifying aspect of death as extinction. For while the "arena" is on its most literal level the tennis court, it is additionally the wearing and memory-laden life of the body:

darkness already in his strokes,
even in death cramps waving an arm back and forth
to the disgust of the night nurse
(to whom the wife whispers, "Well,
at least I always knew where he was!");
and smiling; and a few hours later found dead—
the smile still in place but the ice bag
left on the brow now inexplicably
Scotchtaped to the right elbow—causing
all those bright trophies to slip permanently,
though not in fact much farther, out of reach,
all except the thick-bottomed young man
about to doublefault in soft metal on the windowsill:
"Runner-Up Men's Class B Consolation Doubles
St. Johnsbury Kiwanis Tennis Tournament 1969" . . .

This is a central trope in Kinnell's work, though it has sel-
dom taken such good-natured form. Death is seen not only as
the fate but perhaps even the engine of every life, or if not the
engine somehow the purpose. The present is a sort of window,
normally opaque, but momentarily clear. And through it can
be seen not only the eventuality of the present but the arc
connecting the present with its outcome.

Here are some other examples from *Mortal Acts, Mortal
Words.* Adam and Eve, biting the apple, are seen as

> . . . poisoning themselves
> into the joy
> that has to watch itself go away.

And here are the final three lines of "Memory of Wilmington":

> I was fifteen, I think. Wilmington then
> was far along on its way to becoming a city
> and already well advanced on its way back to dust.

And in "The Rainbow" life in the womb is described as "that
last time we knew / more of happiness than of time."

But this trope has been crucial to Kinnell from the begin-
ning. Here are the first four lines of "Island of Night," the third
poem in *The Avenue Bearing the Initial of Christ into the New World.*

> I saw in a dream a beautiful island
> Surrounded by an abrasive river,
> And soon it was all rubbed into river and
> Gone forever, even the sweet millet and the clover.

But Kinnell's tennis poem is now at its only stanza break, and now physical description begins to give off an aura, a prefiguration of being translated.

> Clouds come over the moon;
> all the lines go out. November last year
> in Lyndonville: it is getting dark,
> snow starts falling, Zander Rubin wobble-twists
> his worst serve out of the black woods behind him,
> Stan Albro lobs into a gust of snow,
> Dan Bredes smashes at where the ball theoretically
> could be coming down . . .

This passage may well begin with a November match last year in Lyndonville when the four men played on into the time after a few first flakes of snow came down. But last year from when? From the time the poem's speaker spoke, one unique time in history, this poem? Or from whatever year a reader finds this poem? Each snowflake has *ubi sunt* neatly lettered on it; these are the snows of yesteryear in advance.

In the moon's absence, only these snows provide natural light against the dark and the black woods. The way the phrase "the lines go out" sounds like "the lights go out" is important. Now it is the knowledge of death that provides us what form provided us earlier, and now we can see, intuitively, that form and convention are outward and visible signs of the knowledge of death.

>   . . . the snow blows down
> and swirls about our legs, darkness flows
> across a disappearing patch of green-painted asphalt
> in the north country, where four men,
> half-volleying, poaching, missing, grunting,
> begging mercy of their bones, hold their ground,
> as winter comes on, all the winters to come.

In his preface to *Walking Down the Stairs,* the book of interviews from which I have quoted so frequently in this brief essay, Kinnell explains what revisions he did and didn't permit himself in traveling from transcriptions of taped interviews toward the printed page.

> I entirely rewrote many perfunctory or muddled answers. A few times when I rewrote answers I found they no longer fit back into their original places. These I put into the interview with Don Bredes and David Brooks, an interview which is partly based on actual conversations, partly a repository of fragments from other interviews, and partly a literary composition.

Surely this is the same Don Bredes who "smashes at where the ball theoretically / could be coming down," and it's pleasant to think of the moment when Kinnell and his interviewers found in the process of putting this particular interview together the ✪ mark where a few words could be gracefully inserted about tennis, the game to which they had given so much energy and excitement, and which had repaid them with an absorbing emblem for the paradoxes of form and freedom, and a durable emblem for how men "hold their ground / as winter comes on, all the winters to come."

(1987)

Personal and Impersonal

A comic strip called "Tips from the Top" used to run on the sports pages. In four panels an always smiling Jack Nicklaus would explain arcane golfing procedures, such as how to hit a four wood out of a fairway bunker from a sidehill lie. What he never described—perhaps the compression of the four-panel format made it impossible—was that the shot was easier to hit for someone who had practiced it six thousand times than for someone who never worried about it until it came up in the course of play. In which case that poor soul was reduced to searching the watery files of memory for the comic strip in which Nicklaus (smiling because he had hit the shot for the six thousandth time long ago in fierce and lonely practice) explained what should be done. In competition, Nicklaus seldom smiles; what we see in his eyes is dry ice.

The practice of a craft suggests the anonymity of apprenticeship, the subjugation of ego to procedures proven valuable by collective and traditional experience.

An apprentice not only learns the tools and materials of a craft, but commits to memory and muscle memory the characteristic motions of an activity. Such repetition is not only a sort of calisthenics. We know that in human evolution greater brain capacity is linked to greater hand-to-eye coordination. Presumably the increasing complexity of physical chores stimulated more complex brain activity. Perhaps lifelong immersion in intricate processes such as writing poetry or playing the piano works similarly.

In any case, an apprentice begins by confronting those parts of a craft that are easiest to describe with words like *anonymous, collective,* and *traditional.* But a skillful apprentice moves toward a condition of mastery by which quite opposite words are invoked: *hallmark, signature, style.*

"You only have so many notes," said Dizzy Gillespie, "and what makes a style is how you get from one note to another."

So the "personal" and the "impersonal" are intricately braided, and thus both difficult and perhaps not even useful to separate, in the way a craft—let's say the craft of poetry—is practiced. But you'd hardly know this from reading and listening to discussions of poetry.

Probably what seems most "personal" to a poet is style, the study of which is, indeed, akin to ballistics.

But what many readers and critics often mean by "personal" is the relationship between poet and subject matter. Can the speaker of the poem be identified with the poet? Does the poem describe a biographically actual, as opposed to an imagined, experience? How much of the emotional temperature of the precipitating impulse of the poem has been retained or lost in the poem? And, to borrow an easy locution from workshop jargon, does the poem "take risks"?

Note that all these questions are 1) *ad hominem* or *ad feminam,* as the case may be; 2) impossible for the reader to answer without information only the poet knows, and thus closer to gossip than to thought; and 3) the equivalent of asking not if an object is useful or beautiful but how much it cost.

In fact we have a hard time thinking, questions of poetry aside, about what constitutes a self, what can be meaningfully termed "personal," what constitutes personality.

One urge we have is to be consistent, coherent, predictable. We long for a nuclear ego. It's to this sense of self the miscreant party-goer refers when he says, apologizing for his behavior, "I wasn't myself." But who was he, then? "You know me," he might begin a hopeful sentence to a friend. He's "a regular guy."

Another urge is to be unpredictable, complex (as Zoot Sims

once said of Stan Getz, "he's a great bunch of guys"), a microcosmic burble of human variety.

We're neither so various nor so consistent in our idea of ourselves as it might please us to think. We're an anthology of selves, and so, inconsistent; but the anthology is chosen by the same editor, and so, consistent. The word *anthology* comes from a Greek word that means bouquet. Perhaps the resolution of different scents into harmony is the most consistency we'll achieve or should strive for.

The narratives we compose (and revise continuously) of our lives are an attempt at such a harmony. But they're not documentaries. "History is what one age finds worthy of note in another," Jacob Burkhardt wrote. The history of an individual is probably similar.

The language we write in is anonymous, collective and traditional, and likely it's with the language itself that we should strike a personal relationship, a style without which content is simply imposed upon us by the massive power of conventional rhetoric and cliché. Too little attention is paid to style as a prophylaxis against cant.

No surprise that we cleave to our autobiographies. At least they belong to us, whereas the language in which we tell such stories belongs—and this is one secret of its trustworthiness—to no one. The same impersonality is also a danger to us, of course: like social insects, we could diligently trace received patterns and find that work sufficient.

As Hebbel wrote, "If language had been the creation, not of poetry, but of logic, we should have only one."

"Originality does not consist of saying what no one has ever said before, but in saying exactly what you think yourself," James Stephen wrote. It turns out this is surprisingly difficult. Perhaps that's why the diction we use in workshops, where we try to help each other do it, is such a Calvinist diction. Does the poem *work*? Does it *earn* its last line? Does it *take risks*?

But all these questions betray an urge to locate the poem's authority in an attitude the poet took toward the poem, to allay the anxiety we feel when we remember that the poem on the page, neither personal nor impersonal but itself, is the only source of whatever authority it has.

Jack Nicklaus didn't hit that shot out of a fairway bunker from a sidehill lie with his personality; he hit it with a four wood.

(1981)

Billie Holiday and Lester Young on "Me, Myself, and I"

June 15, 1937. Holiday had the great Basie rhythm section behind her: Freddie Green, guitar; Walter Page, bass; Jo Jones, drums. Jimmy Sherman was on piano, sitting in for Teddy Wilson, whom producer John Hammond normally used for these sessions, and though Sherman was a less spry and fuzzier-toned pianist than Wilson, on the numbers cut at this session he plays characteristic Wilson figures, as if he knew whom the producer and singer had really wanted. Buck Clayton was on trumpet, Edmund Hall on clarinet, and Lester Young played tenor sax.

Holiday had recorded a first session under her own name in July 1936, and popular demand for her records was sufficient that, eleven months later, she was at her fifth such date. A session might produce two to four numbers for release. Preparation was minimal. The best jazzmen of the time were playing behind her, and most had got their jazz educations playing in well-run bands like Basie's or Benny Goodman's. It was a matter of professional pride for them to come into the studio, check out the head arrangement, run through the piece once or twice, and then record it. This particular session included "A Sailboat in the Moonlight" and "Without Your Love."

"Me, Myself, and I" is a cheerful piece of fluff whose lyrics go like this:

> Me, Myself, and I are all in love with you
> We all think you're wonderful, we do

Me, Myself, and I have just one point of view
We're convinced there's no one else like you
It can't be denied dear, you brought the sun to us
We'd be satisfied, dear, if you'd belong to one of us
If you pass me by, three hearts will break in two
'Cause Me, Myself, and I are all in love with you

What the band does is wait for Lester Young to string together a pair of supple four-bar phrases that weave like a sine curve around the melody, not yet stated, and then vamp quietly while Holiday goes through the lyrics once. The tempo is a jaunty fox trot. This is a young Billie Holiday, at a time when her style was most clearly influenced by Louis Armstrong's singing and before the natural elegance of her phrasing had begun to turn to mannerism. In this recording there's none of the passionate identification she makes with the lyrics of, let's say, her January 1937 version of "I Must Have That Man"; you can feel those lyrics fill with longing and erotic greed as she gets farther and farther into them. These are the lyrics of a pop tune of the day, some hopeful composer's little money-maker, and she skates over them gracefully, for to let much weight fall on such lyrics would buckle them. In her torchier numbers we hear the broken-hearted queen of suffering that hagiography made her, but in numbers like "My, Myself, and I" we hear the great emotional warmth that is her most inimitable characteristic. I think it's the love of making music with great musicians somehow turned into music. Her best work of this period is radiant with pleasure. She had the most rock-steady rhythm section in the history of jazz behind her, and in Young the one musician who shared her ability to play pleasure.

While she's on her way through the lyrics the first time, Clayton plays quietly behind her with his horn muted and Young teams up with Hall to vamp a little, but mostly what we hear is Holiday playing with the rhythmic possibilities of the song, changing pace, coming in ahead or behind the beat, singing with a kind of exuberance that feels like breaking into a run on a beautiful day.

Then she lays out while the front line takes solos. Hall's solo lasts as long as it would take to sing the first four lines of the lyrics. Then Clayton, and Clayton and Sherman together, split the remaining four lines. Hall's tone is a great foil for Young's; Hall is at his best in the middle register of the clarinet. His tone is throaty and has an audible hint of the word *wood* in *woodwind*. Like Young, he tends to improvise on the melody, though Hall sticks closer to it than Young, whose solos are like the melody dreaming about itself. These are short performances, cut well before the LP and so within the three-minute limit of the 78. So everyone's solo is heard in the immediate memory of everyone else's.

Next we hear Clayton, unmuted now, and then Sherman playing a Wilson-like solo but without the lilt and articulate ease with which Wilson would have played it. Wilson's figures sound as if he'd just spoken something and was as happily pleased by what he'd uttered as everyone in his audience; Sherman's sound thought out and carefully worked into a conversation. Yet if you transcribed them in musical notation, you couldn't say surely which man played which. Style is very hard to talk about in jazz, lest you talk of mere personality on the one hand or fall into a stupefied mysticism on the other. But the ear, God bless it, can quickly recognize and grow to understand a style.

Now the lyrics get sung once more, but this time through Lester Young is playing behind Holiday, for his role is an accompanist's. But if he's behind her, he's at her shoulder. Whitney Balliett describes the effect of Holiday and Young together and at their best as "a single voice split in two." Indeed, at this time Young was living with Holiday and her mother, and their interplay is so much like the relaxed erotic banter of lovers that people like to ascribe the music to the relationship rather than to the musicians. But theirs was probably a platonic relationship, and each loved the ease they both found so frequently in music and so seldom anywhere else.

Young loved the smooth in life. "Play vanilla for me," he once upbraided a boisterous drummer. "Nice eyes, no evil spirits," he would offer as a ground rule when contention arose. He often wore slippers on the stand. He smoked marijuana incessantly and was almost always high.

Young's tone was pale and wispy and languidly under-stated. He had none of the burly vibrato or rushing, masculine lyricism of Coleman Hawkins, who ruled the tenor when Lester came on the scene. Young never seemed urgent and could run longer and farther behind the beat than any musician who could also swing, which he never failed to do. There was something piss-elegant and offhand about his style, and because he had about him none of the will and ambition of the pioneer, his contribution to jazz history and his influence are still underestimated. Armstrong and Parker are like forces of nature; Young seems like a force of emotional life, poised as if between the relentlessness of nature and the decisions of civilization. He played with an unmatched tenderness, as if suffering and pleasure were impossible without each other, and why not? A master of mixed feelings, perhaps a slave to them, he mediated beautifully between Holiday's more melodramatic swings from giddiness to pain, and when they worked together in the late thirties, they were continually finishing each other's musical sentences.

This time through the lyrics, Young is rushing ahead while Holiday lags behind. It's one of his most liquid passages and can foster the illusion that music poured from him like water from a glass. His solos are studded with oddly accurate silences, often at the beginning of a phrase. It's as if the listener has come into a sentence halfway through. By the end it will be complete and full of feeling. For the length of time it takes Holiday to sing the eight lines of threadbare lyrics again and Young to play along, all those usual silences in his solos are filled by Holiday singing. At times, she's singing and he's playing, both, like intertwined vines. No wonder people think it's sexy; it is. But it's sexy like the patter of Nick and Nora Charles. More than anything it's about the pleasure of playing together, of sharing a skill. Think how it must feel to be Holiday. Not only can she sing but she has been given the best possible musicians to work with, and the languid guy in slippers is as close to a soulmate, musically, as she'll ever be likely to find. Together they define pleasure in the best possible way—by living it.

(1988)

The Continuity of
James Wright's Poems

By now almost everyone who cares about American poetry knows the story about James Wright's *The Branch Will Not Break* (1963). But like the tale of Abner Doubleday and the invention of baseball, the story is more shapely than true, and its use has been primarily for polemicists. So because I think James Wright has already written a significant body of generous and beautiful poems, and because I think the story distracts us from noticing some of the more important things Wright has actually been doing in developing that body of poetry, I begin my essay-in-tribute by debunking it.

For Robert Bly, writing in the *Sixties* in 1966, *The Branch Will Not Break* signaled an escape. One kind of poetry, influenced by Eliot and Ransom, was a jail. The world is vast, various. "Yet the colleges still understand poetry as a climb into a walled garden."

Writing in the *Nation* in 1963, L. D. Rubin, Jr., had argued—embodying the tunnel vision that drove Bly to distraction—that Wright's book "is a kind of willful refusal to enter into the business of interpreting experience." Implicit in Rubin's diction is the idea of a poet as interpreter for hire. Perhaps the fatigue of writing criticism had so infused Rubin that he imagined in Wright a refusal that Rubin had not been able to make.

To other critics, technical differences were important. *The Green Wall* (1957) and *Saint Judas* (1959) contained primarily poems written in rhyme, metrically regular. *The Branch Will Not Break* did not. Neither did *Shall We Gather at the River* (1968), so that in *Alone with America* (1969), Richard Howard could contend that Wright "had written four volumes of poetry, two in verse and two (it is tempting to say) inversely." And in an interesting appreciative article in the *Georgia Review* in 1973, James Seay says that after Wright's second book, "the poems . . . became less formal."

But surely all poems are formal. They take shape. For them to take a shape relatively unlike the shape of other poems is not the same thing as it is to be informal or inverse.

Bly has written well of one important feature in Wright's early work. The themes for which Wright has been so widely praised since the presumed conversion marked by *The Branch Will Not Break* were present from the beginning. "He has more respect for those who break laws than those who keep them," Bly wrote during our war in Vietnam. Wright is drawn to the dead, the drunk, the defeated. He is interested "not in a poetic grief . . . but in an insupportable grief."

"The Seasonless" is a poem about the dispossessed from *The Green Wall*, written in octosyllabics in a recurring stanza (*ababcdeecd*). The truth is, many of Wright's early poems in traditional forms are not particularly well written. Here is the first stanza of "The Seasonless":

> When snows begin to fill the park,
> It is not hard to keep the eyes
> Secure against the flickering dark,
> Aware of summer ghosts that rise.
> The blistered trellis seems to move
> The memory toward root and rose,
> The empty fountain fills the air
> With spray that spangled women's hair;
> And men who walk this park in love
> May bide the time of falling snows.

This is not good writing. Adjectives like "flickering, summer, empty, falling," all seem predictable, both for their becalmed tone and to fill out the slack sail of the metrics. Throughout the stanza the emotional distance between the speaker and poem is considerable, as emphasized by the verbs "begin, seems, may." An indirect construction like "It is not hard" works similarly. Yet this emotional distance serves no purpose in the poem, which strives to be about the speaker's identification with these lonely men. Indeed, in the fourth stanza, "lonely underneath a heap / Of overcoat and crusted ice, / A man goes by, and looks for sleep." I think this man is the speaker of the poem. "Nothing about his face revives / A longing to evade the cold." Wright's distrust of consolation is one of the things I love most in his poems. But there is something too neat and summary about these two lines, as if they explained not something in the poem, but the poet's attitude toward the poem.

And after these two lines the poem closes with four more:

> The night returns to keep him old,
> And why should he, the lost and lulled,
> Pray for the night of vanished lives,
> The day of girls blown green and gold?

It is as if writing in a form that has been so well used by masters of English poetry makes it almost impossible for Wright not to load his lines with echoes, including those echoes of a general tone that produce a prettily blurred sound. "The night returns to keep him old" is noisily significant, but doesn't, actually, make sense. Can the night go away? Given that time goes on, can anyone be kept old or young? The specific echoes in the last line—of Housman, of Frost's "Nothing Gold Can Stay"—are so loud they constitute a failure of tact and proportion, and the line is difficult to read as anything but an echo.

I spend so much time on an early poem I don't like in order to suggest that Wright did not abandon, in a dramatic move similar to religious conversion, an early career as a glib poet in traditional forms. Like most young poets, he began in the currently accepted style. I think not only that he found it wanting, but also that it found him wanting. Comparing his early poems, let's say, to Richard Wilbur's, we see that Wright used traditional forms clumsily. To use a period style well, one has to fight its habits, which are often bad habits and are certainly bad in that they are the habits of others. And to find in a period style those elements that are genuinely and usefully traditional is a complex enterprise. I believe that Wright is a profoundly traditional poet, but that he discovered his personal uses for literary tradition through rhetorical forms, rather than through stanza forms or rhyming patterns.

Many of his rhetorical forms come from the King James Bible, both in its official and written form as Scripture, and in its unofficial and oral form as evangelists' spiels, florid persuasion. In these models the Word and the word are close. Another model is plain talk, which is direct, colloquial, confessional; here fancy language is a likely sign of insincerity, and Wright's declared use of E. A. Robinson and Frost as models makes sense as an attempt to reconcile his love and suspicion of rhetoric.

The poem "At the Executed Murderer's Grave," from *Saint Judas*, exhibits as well as any poem from this stage of Wright's career the war between rhetorical and stanza models. The poem is in iambic pentameter, and its metrical pressures cause some bad mangles. Here are the first four lines:

> My name is James A. Wright, and I was born
> Twenty-five miles from this infected grave,
> In Martins Ferry, Ohio, where one slave
> To Hazel-Atlas Glass became my father.

The first line is fine, and gives us the sense, typical in Wright, that to be born is to die in order to be born again. "Infected" strikes a prophet's note (Isaiah, I guess, would be the prophet Wright reads most avidly). But the inversion in lines three and four is ugly and metrically awkward. It is rough-hewn enough to be sincere, if sincerity is measured by a certain retraction from glossy skill. But paying attention to roughing up the lines, on the one hand, and to the measure by which we judge them rough or smooth, on the other, reveals a divided attention. And Wright's urge is to be whole.

> Earth is a door I cannot even face.
> Order be damned, I do not want to die,
> Even to keep Belaire, Ohio, safe.

In a later poem, I think, Wright would have written "a door I cannot face." The "even" is filler. But not "can't" for "cannot." And these lines bring the poem close to a central imaginative problem for Wright. The earth is lovely and it lives by death. What can we do with such knowledge?

To say that Wright's language grows at once simpler and more successfully formal is to go upstream against the implications of Bly, Rubin, Howard, and Seay. To talk of prose style in such terms would surprise nobody. Dialogue in Hemingway is both "simple" and "formal," and Nabokov's elaborately "formal" rendering of Lolita's simplicities is one of the glories of American fiction. But in reference to poetry, such terms are too often assumed to be contradictory. I don't understand why. To see a sonnet as more "formal" than a list in Whitman is to believe an ocelot more formal than a lizard. Neither am I interested in imagining which animal is more "organic."

The poems in *The Branch Will Not Break* and *Shall We Gather at the River,* and the poems in Wright's subsequent *Two Citizens* (1973), continue his characteristic themes. We see the faded, the defeated, the dead. And for everyone, a vast loneliness. In one poem Wright tells us that "the sea . . . once solved the whole loneliness / Of the midwest." For loneliness to be both whole and soluble is a paradox central to Wright's imagination.

But Wright's style had changed, becoming both more plain and more formal. It reminds me as much of Sherwood Anderson's prose as it does of any poet. Here is a passage from a letter Anderson wrote to a son who was a young painter.

> The object of art is not to make salable pictures. It is to save yourself.
> Any clearness I have in my own life is due to my feeling for words.
> The fools who write articles about me think that one morning I suddenly decided to write and began to produce masterpieces.
> There is no special trick about writing or painting either. I wrote constantly for fifteen years before I produced anything with solidity to it.
> For days, weeks, and months, now I can't do it.

You saw me in Paris this winter. I was in a dead blank time.
You have to live through such times all your life.
The thing, of course, is to make yourself alive. Most people
remain all of their lives in a stupor.
The point of being an artist is that you may live.

I'm reminded of these lines from "She's Awake," in *Two Citizens*.

For God's sake, wake up, how in hell am I going to die?

It was easy.
All I had to do was delete the words lonely and shadow,
Dispose of the dactylic hexameters in amphibrachs
Gather your lonely life into my life,
And love your life.

Another poem in *Two Citizens*, "The Old WPA Swimming Pool
in Martins Ferry, Ohio," ends:

I have loved you all this time
And didn't even know
I am alive.

I think that for Wright the object of art *is* to save yourself, and
the point of being an artist is that you may live.

The passage from Anderson also reminds me of Wright because
it is in the plain style. Anderson can write a sentence like
"I was in a dead blank time" only by deleting the words *lonely*
and *shadow*. Wright has worked hard to make such deletions.
Bly complained, justifiably, I think, that in *The Branch Will Not
Break*, "even the ants are well-read." In that book we find lines
like

Mother of roots, you have not seeded
The tall ashes of loneliness
For me. Therefore,
Now I go.

The same poem ("Goodbye to the Poetry of Calcium") ends:

> Look, I am nothing.
> I do not even have ashes to rub into my eyes.

In *Collected Poems* (1971), Wright included a selection of his translations (from Jimenez, Guillen, Neruda, Trakl, Vallejo, Salinas, and Goethe) between *Saint Judas* and *The Branch Will Not Break*. A translator can bring over into his own language the denotative level of a poem and its physical imagery. But tonal and textural peculiarities in the poem are in the language—we might almost say *of* the language—in which it was written. They can't be detached from it. The average translator stops here. Wright is a good translator, and invents for his English versions devices to produce an effect in the reader that feels something like the way the poem in the original felt to Wright. But even when a good translator is at work, his version is usually slightly less complicated, tonally and texturally, than the original poem. So that when Wright was working on these translations and producing English versions simpler than the poems in his own first two books, he may well have taken courage in his struggle for a plain style in his own poems. Certainly lines like

> Look: I am nothing.
> I do not even have ashes to rub into my eyes

are better, cleaner, and embody clearer emotions, than almost any lines from the first two books.

Translating can influence a poet in other ways. In English we indicate whether a genitive construction is subjective or objective by word order; in Romance languages this is done by inflection. So in a Romance language a genitive can sometimes be ambiguous, either subjective or objective. To translate the phrase into colloquial English would require resolving the ambiguity. It would either be the roots' mother or a mother made of roots. To preserve the ambiguity a translator says "mother of roots." Now, that phrase is Wright's own. But it was after he made many of his translations that he began to use the *of* construction frequently in his poems. Its effect is compression. The poem "Twilights" ends with a single line set off as a separate stanza:

> A red shadow of steel mills.

In that line the compression and ambiguity are effective. But in "mother of roots" and "tall ashes of loneliness," because the whole passage is not principally written to evoke a complicated mood or perception (as "a red shadow of steel mills" is), but in part to advance an argument, the ambiguity is an impediment.

There are passages in the translations included in *Collected Poems* that must have given Wright special excitement to translate, for they spoke, in their varying accents, in nearly the way he would come to speak in his own. Here's the end of Wright's version of Pedro Salinas's "Not in Marble Palaces":

> That's why our life
> doesn't appear to be lived:
> slippery, evasive,
> it left behind neither wakes
> nor footprints. If you want
> to remember it, don't look
> where you always look for traces
> and recollections.
> Don't look at your soul,
> your shadow or your lips.
> Look carefully into the palm
> of your hand, it's empty.

I greatly prefer these lines to George Trakl's "Sleep," in Wright's version:

> Not your dark poisons again,
> White sleep!
> This fantastically strange garden
> Of trees in deepening twilight
> Fills up with serpents, nightmoths,
> Spiders, bats.
> Approaching the stranger! Your abandoned shadow
> In the red of evening
> Is a dark pirate ship

On the salty oceans of confusion.
White birds from the outskirts of the night
Flutter out over the shuddering cities
Of steel.

Everything in the poem smells, to me, of shopworn poetic grief. The garden isn't so fantastically strange, after all; it is made from Halloween props. And the *of* constructions are telling. The "salty oceans of confusion" is paraphrastic, and "the outskirts of the night" portentously poetic. The emotional tone of the poem should be fragile, but everything is crude, black or white, in heavy outline.

Trakl's influence, in the story about *The Branch Will Not Break,* liberated in Wright an ability to use images to refer directly to intense emotions, indeed to create those emotions in the reader rather than refer the reader to those emotions. But Trakl's influence, or whatever combination of Wright's instincts the phrase "Trakl's influence" points to, also provided Wright with a new form for struggling against his taste for fancy writing.

Here is "The Jewel," from *The Branch Will Not Break.*

There is this cave
In the air behind my body
That nobody is going to touch:
A cloister, a silence   ·
Closing around a blossom of fire.
When I stand upright in the wind,
My bones turn to dark emeralds.

In an essay in *Field* in 1973, Wright says that while "the great poets write their books in secret, we discover their books openly." I think he might say, as well, that we live our lives in secret, whether we are great poets or not poets at all, and that if we are lucky and generous a few people love us openly. So the first three lines of "The Jewel" are wonderful to me. Lines 1 and 3 play off a kind of speech I heard and spoke as a boy in Ohio. I can hear a boy's mock-defiance in "That nobody is going to touch," and in the casual "There is this cave" I hear the offhanded beginning often used to introduce some important topic. The second line is strange. A cave is air shaped by walls, but this cave is shaped by air. This space, this solitude Wright speaks of, is palpable but immaterial.

But the last four lines of the poem are fancy writing. There is something heraldic about the cloister, the blossom of fire, and the bones turned to dark emeralds. One almost expects a unicorn.

I think the poem is about whether or not its speaker is worthy to be loved, and that the cave serves both as a space to which he may retreat if unworthy, and also as an impediment to those forms of love—probably the only valuable forms—in which it is crucial not to hedge your bets. The poem puts the issue starkly, and the fancy writing of the last four lines is a way to turn away from that starkness and its challenge.

In *Shall We Gather at the River* Wright has a remarkable poem, a prayer called "Speak."

> To speak in a flat voice
> Is all that I can do.
> I have gone every place
> Asking for you.
> Wondering where to turn
> And how the search would end
> And the last streetlight spin
> Above me blind.
>
> Then I returned rebuffed
> And saw under the sun
> The race not to the swift
> Nor the battle won.
> Liston dives in the tank,
> Lord, in Lewiston, Maine,
> And Ernie Doty's drunk
> In hell again.
>
> And Jenny, oh my Jenny
> Whom I love, rhyme be damned,
> Has broken her spare beauty
> In a whorehouse old.
> She left her new baby
> In a bus-station can,
> And sprightly danced away
> Through Jacksontown.

Which is a place I know,
One where I got picked up
A few shrunk years ago
By a good cop.
Believe it, Lord, or not.
Don't ask me who he was.
I speak of flat defeat
In a flat voice.

I have gone forward with
Some, a few lonely some.
They have fallen to death.
I die with them.
Lord, I have loved Thy cursed,
The beauty of Thy house:
Come down. Come down. Why dost
Thou hide thy face?

Wright here associates a flat voice with defeat. So that a round voice, or a fancy style, is for the lies a man may tell himself if he should hope for victory, or justification. It is the voice a man uses to cheer himself, to tell himself that there is earthly justice (the race to the swift). But in this poem there is no earthly justice, no consolation, and what fancy writing there is consists in taking on the accents and rhythms of religious dialogue, because the language of prayer and the language of the King James Bible are plain and formal.

The plain style also turns out to be the language for rejoicing. *Two Citizens* begins with a curse for America (just as *Shall We Gather at the River*, after a preface poem, begins with a curse for Minneapolis), and ends with ecstatic love poems. In the last of these Wright says,

No, I ain't much.
The one tongue I can write in
Is my Ohioan.

And the book's epigraph—a primary example of plain speech in writing—is from Hemingway's "The Killers."

127

"Well, bright boy," Max said, looking into the mirror, "why don't you say something?"

"What's it all about?"

"Hey, Al," Max called, "bright boy want to know what it's all about."

"Why don't you tell him?" Al's voice came from the kitchen.

"What do you think it's all about?"

"I don't know."

"What do you think?"

In "A Poem of Towers" Wright says "Wise and foolish / Both are gone." The defeat in "Speak" has been by *Two Citizens* transformed into a cleared ground, a place to begin from, or just to walk around.

In Wright's earlier poems the Midwest is whole and lonely because every citizen is alone (thus whole, in that diminished sense), and with no links between citizens there can be no body politic, and no real citizenship. Everyone is atomic.

In *Two Citizens* Wright uses the word *alone* in a new way, to mean two lovers by themselves. "And me there alone at last with my only love, / Waiting to begin."

It's interesting to compare "The Young Good Man" from *Two Citizens* with "An Offering for Mr. Bluehart," one of the best poems in *Saint Judas*.

Mr. Bluehart owned an orchard from which the poem's speaker and some friends stole fruit; he had driven them away with gunfire.

> Sorry for him, or any man
> Who lost his labored wealth to thieves,
> Today I mourn him, as I can,
> By leaving in their golden leaves
> Some luscious apples overhead.
> Now may my abstinence restore
> Peace to the orchard and the dead.
> We shall not nag them anymore.

Two stanzas precede this final one, but it isn't until four lines from the poem's end that we know what kind of fruit the boys stole. The terms are economic ("restore," "lost his labored wealth to thieves") and allegorical ("leaving in the golden leaves / Some luscious apples overhead"). The prayer is to reverse a fall: "Now may my abstinence restore / Peace to the orchard and the dead."

But in "The Young Good Man," a poem in three parts, whose second section I quote here, the speaker (Wright, himself, as the book insists) has been warned by "everybody I knew, loved and respected" that the wild crab apples "taste so bitter you pucker / Two days at least."

> I don't know why,
> One evening in August something illuminated my body
> And I got sick of laying my cold
> Hands on myself.
> I lied to my family I was going for a walk uptown.
>
> When I got to that hill,
> Which now, I hear, Bluehart has sold to the Hanna
> Strip Mine Company, it was no trouble at all to me.
> Within fifteen yards of that charged fence I found me
> A wild crab apple.
>
> I licked it all over.
> You are going to believe this.
> It tasted sweet.
>
> I know what would have happened to my tongue
> If I had bitten. The people who love me
> Are sure as hell no fools.

Many of Wright's poems are about forgiveness, and many of his early poems are haunted by the possibility that none of us deserves love and we are therefore fools to love anyone. Throughout *Two Citizens* everyone is forgiven before the poems begin, even Wright himself. In a joyful passage from "The Streets Grow Young" he parodies the guilt-ridden man's willingness to seek crimes large enough to justify his guilt.

> Okay. I accept your forgiveness.
> I started the Reichstag fire.

I invented the ball-point pen.
I ate the British governor of Rhodesia.

(But that was a long time ago,
And I thought he was assorted fruits and chicken sauce.
Still, all the same.)

Okay now, hit the road, and leave me
And my girl alone.

A similar exalted giddiness makes the book's love poems wonderfully believable and lighthearted.

What have I got to do?
The sky is shattering,
The plain sky grows so blue.
Some day I have to die,
As everyone must do
Alone, alone, alone,
Peaceful as peaceful stone.
You are the earth's body.
I will die on the wing.
To me you are everything
That matters, chickadee.
You live so much in me.
Chickadees sing in the snow.
I will die on the wing,
I love you so.

Even Wright's love-running feud with the dead is behind him in this book.

And in his 1973 essay in *Field* Wright talks about his relationship to poetic tradition. Bothered by some bad polemical writing on free verse (perhaps he has been bothered, too, by some versions of the story about *The Branch Will Not Break*), he complains that "the theory of our current free verse involves a complete rejection of the past." Of course the practice of "free verse" does not, as Wright well knows.

I put "free verse" in quotes because I, too, am bothered by its similarity to a political slogan (Free Huey). Too much talk about poetics is really talk about politics in disguise. One bad polemic relishes William Carlos Williams's remark that the sonnet is a fascist form because it makes the words run on time. An opposite bad polemic equates traditional verse forms with established social, religious, and political orders. Such discussion seems to me both stupid and confusing.

Wright is speaking, in his essay in *Field*, out of what he knows about how a poet learns to write better. Slowly, as Sherwood Anderson was right to say. I think that we work hard to learn what little we learn, and that we learn almost all of it from the past.

Wright recognizes that it is a long and intricate enterprise to forge a personal relationship to literary tradition. The triumph of *Two Citizens* is that he has done so. The openness in that book and in the pieces he's published since has little to do, I'm sure, with open or closed forms, whatever they may be. It is a spiritual quality, which Wright learned to register in a language that is partly Ohioan, partly King James Bible and Billy Sunday, and partly a distillation from those poets in our literary tradition who mattered most personally to Wright.

Each of the books Wright has given us contains wonderful and memorable poems. We have no right to ask more of a poet, but our important poets ask more of themselves. It is such a vocation, such a calling, that I have tried to trace in these notes. I believe that Wright's great achievement so far has been to imagine the language in which he can make the simple assertions—though they are, since Wright is a religious poet, as basic as they are simple—of *Two Citizens*. It is as if, having made the language for himself, Wright wanted first to test it against the barest propositions: *I love you,* or *It is a beautiful day.* To expand the range and complexity of what he will say in his restored language will be, I expect, his next task, and it will be our privilege to watch him continue.

(1977)

131

Ignorance

We like to talk about poetry as a form of knowledge, a way of knowing, as if it were good to be knowing. In the science fiction movies of the 1950s and 1960s, made in the stunned calm aftermath of the split atom, once the radiation-swollen monsters have been vanquished and the hero and heroine can pause for deep breath and thought, one of them is bound to say to the other that there are some things humans are not meant to know. But Pandora's box is to open.

And Pandora's box is to suffer opening. It is not accidental that such atomic- and, later, hydrogen-nightmare movies were made almost exclusively in America and Japan.

In Roger Corman's 1963 film, *The Man with the X-ray Eyes*, Ray Milland could see through the surfaces of things to their structures. He had conducted experiments on himself, against the advice of more cautious but drably conventional colleagues, to get this ability. Once won, it destroyed him. He was, to cite a Hitchcock title, "The Man Who Knew Too Much," which is a morally melodramatic Hollywood way to say "the man who knew dangerous things." It's not the quantity of what he knew that was a problem but that he exceeded limits and broke taboos.

In one scene in the movie Milland is riding in a car. Modern buildings whir by. He wears sunglasses, the bright light of geometrical structure hurts his eyes so, and his heart and soul. It's like taking Blake for a spin around Houston; Newton has crushingly won the day. The world seems to be made of blueprints, and the structural principles for all the buildings are plagiarisms—not of some historic source, but of each other.

Milland's living hell has no surfaces: it turns out that beauty *is* only skin deep. Isn't it the light on the lawn that we love, and not the moles, the industrious worms, the fine hairlets of roots? Does a poem really have, as the textbooks say, "levels" of meaning (seven, like Troy!)? Or isn't what is miraculous about poems that they are only ink on paper, the way we live only on the surface of the earth, and the way lovers have, finally, only the surfaces of each other's bodies?

It's true, the viewer feels by the end of Corman's stylishly tawdry movie, that the Ray Milland character gave up everything valuable. At the end of the movie he takes off his sunglasses, and the screen, doused with light, goes bright white, as if blindness were, after all, too much light, the saturating flash of the split atom.

Here is an A. E. Housman poem.

> Crossing alone the nighted ferry
> With the one coin for fee,
> Whom, on the wharf of Lethe waiting,
> Count you to find? Not me.
>
> The brisk, fond lackey to fetch and carry,
> The true, sick-hearted slave,
> Expect him not in the just city
> And free land of the grave.

The first quatrain is so clumsily written there must be a reason, though not necessarily a good reason, for it. The gawkiness is especially puzzling, since Housman is a poet of glib effects.

The main clause of the convoluted first sentence begins (with its direct object) in line three, but six words (among them the sentence's second present participle) intervene before we get, first the verb, and next the subject, and then another verb in infinitive form, no less unfinished thereby than *crossing* and *waiting* were. Everything is up in the air grammatically and down in the underworld dramatically; time holds its breath. The grammar "imitates," a certain species of poetry handbook would say, the psychological situation. Is this the imitative fallacy? A kind of grammatical onomatopoeia?

As is so often the case, critical terminology creates new problems as fast as it solves old ones. There's a tension the lines can't quite accommodate, between the need of grammar to make knowledge from experience, and the need of experience to resist resolution into knowledge. This tension represents an accuracy, insofar as we imagine for poetry a relationship between knowledge and experience like that between a realistic painting and a landscape. And this tension represents a failure of making, insofar as we imagine for poetry a need for transmutation by which a poem becomes an experience, rather than a report of experience anterior to the poem. Of course poetry won't sit still (D'Annunzio: "Anatomy presupposes a corpse") for this kind of talk, which is why we love and need it.

The second stanza is like the Housman poems we remember more readily than this atypical and interesting one. There's a contest in it, between Housman's classical education and utterly romantic sensibility, and the contest is poised. It's smoother and more "well written." But both stanzas are about the same thing. Here is a love in which the speaker is a slave, a lackey, fond (the word suggests dotage, sexual sentimentality, and ineffectuality, all three at once), a kind of romantic pack animal; he hates it but can't have his love without it. It's one of the last things for him, the way love and death get intertwined when lovers can't imagine a future they can trust. You'll miss me when I'm gone, he seems to be taunting, who won't go until called. Death would make the two lovers finally equal, but it has been the contest for equality on which they have built their love. No less than death, such a love has one coin only. When the debts are cleared, in an ironic City of God, then the struggles of love are replaced by the good citizenship of moral victory and the loss of the wracked body.

I've paraphrased and elaborated, at a length far greater than Housman's poem, what the speaker "knows" about his situation. It isn't knowledge that translates readily to action, unless death be considered an action. The poem is also hollow threat, and loving invective. It's a kind of knowledge—the poem is neither mute nor stupid. But it's a kind of brave ignorance, too.

The poem reminds me of a definition of poetry by Eliot, whom we conventionally think one of our more cerebral poets. Poetry tells us "what it feels like." At just this point in musing about poetry and knowledge we could close down our curiosity by a trick of definition. We could say that "what it feels like" is itself a kind of knowledge, and smugly return to the platitude—half-true, according to the habit of platitudes—that poetry is a kind of knowledge (But "Money, too, is a kind of poetry," as Stevens said, and what does money know?). Knowledge about what? Poetry is "about" our experience, we could say, but it is made out of language. In poetry, experience has some of the intractability of matter. We don't know surely what it is and we know only a little about what use to make of it. And in poetry, language has some of the elusiveness and danger of energy, and likewise its own ineluctable laws.

Two passages from *The Aeneid* (in Allen Mandelbaum's translation) will suggest how much larger the scope of brave ignorance can be. If this were a contest between Housman and Virgil, we could complain about loaded dice. An epic can and had damn well better take on more than an eight-line lyric, and one of these poets is vastly more capable than the other. Each did what he could, and that's beside the point. In Housman's poem we find a vividly animated psychology, in which all its context must be, whether because Housman confined himself to eight lines or because his talent expired at the end of eight lines, "understood," as we used to say of missing parts of speech when we diagrammed sentences. Virgil is explicit.

In book 5 of *The Aeneid*, during the war games, there is a contest between Entellus and the far younger Dares.

> Entellus, rising, stretched his right hand high;
> but Dares, quick to see the coming blow,
> had slipped aside and dodged with his quick body.
> Entellus spent his strength upon the wind;
> his own weight, his own force, had carried him
> heavy, and heavily, with his huge hulk
> down to the ground; just as at times a hollow
> pine, torn up from its roots on Erymathus

or on the slopes of giant Ida, falls.
The Trojan and Sicilian boys leap up;
their shouting takes the sky; and first Acestes
runs to the ring; with pity he lifts up
his friend, as old as he is. But the hero,
not checked and not to be delayed, returns
more keenly to the bout, his anger spurs
his force. His shame, his knowledge of his worth
excite his power; furiously he
drives Dares headlong over all the field,
and now his right hand doubles blows and now
his left; he knows no stay or rest; just as
storm clouds that rattle thick hail on the roofs,
so do the hero's two hands pummel, pound
at Dares, blow on blow, from every side.

Some of this is conventional battle stuff, but there is always in Virgil powerful interaction between action and comment, figure and ground, the conventions he observes and the torque by which he transforms them into components of a personal style. In such a poet, everything can be conventional and simultaneously thick with recognizably personal style.

"Entellus spent his strength upon the wind" is a formulaic line, but the wind is no less real for that. Entellus is about to make a comeback—force spurred by anger and power excited by "his shame, his knowledge of his worth." These could be two distinct items in a series of two, or they could be apposite, so that "knowledge of his worth" becomes a definition of "shame." Virgil's is a tragic and meditative psychology, not merely a dramatized one.

Entellus is a storm, who "knows no stay or rest; just as / storm clouds that rattle thick hail on the roofs, / so do the hero's two hands pummel, pound / at Dares, blow on blow, from every side." Again and again in *The Aeneid* what seems to be outside us, and thus susceptible to prediction and control, enters us, the way weather in this passage enters Entellus. Mandelbaum's translation acutely renders the gathering speed of this process: blows are doubled by the right *and* left hand and then we get "stay or rest," and then "pummel, pound," and then "blow on blow," until this ferocity, doubling (like rhetorical momentum) at a geometrical rather than an arithmetical pace, surrounds us "from every side" with a hail of shame and worth and anger. Perhaps what it means to be "taken by storm" is to weather the full force of our ignorance; if so, ignorance is not merely a lack, but a passion.

The Aeneid is about love and war, fixed sentimentally in our time as alternatives by the injunction to make love and not war. The avoidance of the harsh word "but" in the formula tells us much about the ways we wanted to be moved when that phrase seemed like an epigram. If history has made war so repellent that we have trouble with the imaginative fusion Virgil made of love and war, that is a possible good omen for our politics, and when we need to remember how much of love is aggression, we can find our texts in Freud, so long as we don't shrink "love and war" to "love and anger." But it is we who want to sunder love and war.

The Aeneid continually links them. In book 8 Venus, fearful for her son, Aeneas, intercedes with her husband Vulcan. They are gods, and therefore they are the weather of humans, the way parents are the weather of children. But they are gods made in our image, and therefore they are themselves subject to weather.

In this passage Venus is "the goddess," and "he" is Vulcan, the blacksmith, so the flame is his own petard.

> The goddess spoke; and as he hesitates,
> with snow-white arms on this side and on that
> she warms him in a soft embrace. At once
> he caught the customary flame; familiar
> heat reached into his marrow, riding through
> his agitated bones—just as at times
> a streak of fire will rip through flashing thunder
> and race across the clouds with glittering light.
> His wife, rejoicing in her craftiness
> and conscious of her liveliness, sensed this.

Here the storm is habitual desire. Her arms are only two, and they come "on this side and on that," but we sense the power of desire that is "customary" and "familiar" (it is desire that includes a family, and thus her son, and his), and know how Vulcan is surrounded (he is doubly surrounded, in fact: not only is desire "around" him, like Venus's arms, but it is also spreading from the inside out, from the marrow). Sexual love makes us weather, so that we are the storm, the weight of our bodies and the diffusion of the air, both, just as we are love and war, both, fighting by love for a way to continue what love has made valuable to each of us. In short, the whole weight of time, as humans know it, is on us, and what time feels like; it is the need to have time be a central character in such poems as *The Aeneid* that gives us so many scenes in which the gods and humans intersect at pained cost to all parties.

Perhaps to be knowing is to withhold, to hoard knowledge. Eventually knowledge must be spent, or how else could one demonstrate possession of it? But it may be that we never know something so thrillingly as when we can, but have not yet chosen to, disclose it.

"Morality is self-evident," wrote Freud (who also wrote in *The Interpretation of Dreams* a sentence beginning "Personally I haven't had an anxiety dream in years . . ."), but what is self-evident is paradoxically difficult to discover, because it's not self-evident until it's seen.

At a recent dinner I heard someone say of a couple we all—all of us at the table—knew, "Everybody knows they're split up."

Let's stop to think about this short sentence, which doesn't mean what it says or say what it means. If everybody knew it, why say it? "Everybody" means "everybody in the know," and then the sense of the sentence is tautological: "everybody in the know, knows." Perhaps the structure of tautology accounts for what is audibly smug and self-enclosed in this sentence.

By extension, the sentence asks "Are you an everybody or a nobody?" Note how being an individual is excluded from the possibilities. One of us at the table was by this measurement a nobody, and since she was also a close friend to both members of the couple, she was alarmed for their pains, and she was hurt not to have heard even bad news about their lives from them before she heard it as gossip. You may have guessed already how this anecdote will finish. Later that night she phoned them, and woke them up, and what everybody knew was wrong.

I leave it to you to wonder if the moral of that anecdote is self-evident. The role I had in it leaves me few rights to wisdom. But here's what I propose: it's no better in poetry to be knowing than in civilian life, and it's as valuable to be explicit. For whatever you think you know—and you can be explicit about what you don't know—you don't know what you need to learn.

A writer who speaks of having something to say is almost always doomed by that obligation to bad writing, unless he or she is willing to append: "but I don't yet know what it is."

Here, from "Dry Salvages" in Eliot's *Four Quartets*, is a passage about what it can't say.

> For most of us, there is only the unattended
> Moment, the moment in and out of time,
> The distraction fit, lost in a shaft of sunlight,
> The wild thyme unseen, or the winter lightning
> Or the waterfall, or music heard so deeply
> That it is not heard at all, but you are the music
> While the music lasts.

To advertise "a passage about what it can't say" is to boast and disclaim at once. Taken as a whole, the *Four Quartets* could be said to be a poem about certain powerful psychological recurrences, and what great sense certain religious assumptions can make of those recurrences. And so as a whole long poem, the quartets raise questions of belief, at least tangentially, and face the dilemma (the analogy of musical structure is, I think, only a partial answer to the dilemma) of needing to return again and again to the psychological cruxes in order to activate the religious impulse. There is a sort of erotic compulsion, a continual recreation of a powerful and mythological early scenario, in the poem.

But now we are looking at a brief excerpt only, and its

argument, that we find it hard to be vividly present in our lives, and sense in a muffled and insulated way what we both fear and long to undergo more powerfully, is not a specifically religious matter. Where Eliot may be writing nonsense is when he speaks of "music heard so deeply / that it is not heard at all."

In logic, paradox is a way of giving up, of signing that the road ends here. I am not sure that I have ever had a paradoxical emotion, in the sense that an absolute equality between the weight of opposites obtains in a paradox. It may be that emotions don't come in opposites, but that "mixed feelings," as we gingerly call them, always contain some of each other. It seems to me possible that paradox is a way to acknowledge that logic, in order to be a useful faculty, must choose internal consistency rather than inclusiveness, when that choice is confronted, and simultaneously a way of saying that the choice is now confronted. Either the investigation gets carried on by other forms of curiosity, or is abandoned.

Eliot pushes on a little way only, but he writes so well in situations where what might conventionally be called subject matter is all fog and wisp that he knows how to do it, to give weight to both his ignorance and his longing to know. And "but you are the music / While the music lasts" is a magisterial stroke that galvanizes the whole passage; it's interesting to notice that until its very end, the whole sentence is slack and ungathered. It's when Eliot doesn't turn back, but pushes on into his ignorance, that the sentence grows taut and shapely.

"What," wrote R. P. Blackmur, "should we get rid of our ignorance, the very substance of our lives, merely in order to understand one another?"

James Wright's posthumously published book of poems, *This Journey,* has among its many beauties a wonderful poem called "The Vestal in the Forum."

In the 1950s our poetry was awash with poems on Italian statues and fountains written by poets holding a Prix de Rome or a Guggenheim, and the usual percentage held: few of them were good. So in the 1960s—the same decade in which Wright began publishing poems in a plain style, whose knowledge was hidden in, and sometimes by, metaphor—in the 1960s there was a knowing joke in poetry life about how bad conventional poems about Italian statues and fountains were, as if the opportunity rather than the poems were dull.

It is typical of Wright's poetic strengths that he would, in a style hard-won and won partially by rebellion against the literary mannerisms of the 1950s which had most influenced him, rescue the emotional occasion. He is looking at a Roman statue.

> This morning I do not despair
> For the impersonal hatred that the cold
> Wind seems to feel
> When it slips fingers into the flaws
> Of lovely things men made,
> The shoulders of a stone girl
> Pitted by winter.
> Not a spring passes but the roses
> Grow stronger in their support of the wind,
> And now they are conquerors,
> Not garlands any more,
> Of this one face:
> Dimming,
> Clearer to me than most living faces.
> The slow wind and the slow roses
> Are ruining an eyebrow here, a mole there.
> But in this little while
> Before she is gone, her very haggardness
> Amazes me. A dissolving
> Stone, she seems to change from stone to something
> Frail, to someone I can know, someone
> I can almost name.

Among the "lovely things men made" are not only statues but the models for statues, humans in their bodies. Wright was dwindling to death from cancer when he wrote this poem. The poem's own "cold wind" is partly the poem's matter-of-fact tone, the ability Wright prayed for in an earlier poem, "to speak in a plain voice." Plain, in this context, means without the mediation of rhetoric. But also it means surely, stripped cruelly of flesh, eroded, pitted, cracked, on the way from the specific voluptuousness of flesh to the spare, skeletal, democratic shape the dying share. It's the shape time wins from us, even in statues which are by convention immune to time in ways no specific and beloved body can be. But posterity is not breath, and the urban chemistry of Rome is rotting statues and buildings faster than classical time or cold breath could dream of, if they dreamed. The Man with the X-ray Eyes sees death, "clearer to me than most living faces." Than *most* living faces, he takes care to say, rather than pretend he can, like the roses, "grow stronger in support of the wind." I love and recommend the poem's last sentence especially.

> A dissolving
> Stone, she seems to change from stone to something
> Frail, to someone I can know, someone
> I can almost name.

What can be known is frail, and naming is not knowing. We love, we writers, the literary implications of Adam naming the animals in Eden, with their celebration of the power of names and the centrality of language to human knowledge and authority. Language is also central to human confusion and impotence, and Adam in Eden is also a vast baby hurling syllables from his playpen.

John Hollander has a poem, "Adam's Task," based on Genesis 2:20, and here are names of some animals in that poem's world, in which we also live: *glurd, spotted glurd, whitestep, implex, verdle, McFleery's pomma, grawl* (three types of these), *flisket, pambler, greater wherret* and *lesser wherret, sproal, zant, lilyeater,* and (tellingly) *comma-eared mashawk.* Here is a creation made from language rather than from mud and fire and language and clouds of swirling water.

In such a world as the one Hollander ingeniously and somewhat reluctantly, even tenderly, satirizes, most of our nostrums about "creative writing" are true. "No tears in the writer, no tears in the reader," wrote Frost, who may have meant by this maxim that the poet didn't suffer enough to earn any suffering in a reader, or may have meant simply, "Damn, this is a dull party." It isn't, I want to insist, what the poet earns or knows, but what he or she writes, that matters. "No surprise for the writer, no surprise for the reader," Frost went on to say, compounding a nonsense. I don't mean to suggest he wasn't addressing a serious and interesting truth about poems: they somehow contain traces of the urgency with which they were written, and this fact provides both poet and reader with opportunities (though they are different opportunities) for self regard.

And we have silly urgencies. We surprise ourselves over and over with ordinary things, a way both to maintain our sense of wonder and to maintain our deeply narcissistic definitions of pleasure. Hollander's poem exercises his love of language and his love of its limitations by intertwining them, as if the tree of knowledge grew the fruit of ignorance. Probably it does.

Wright's poem ends, because it followed faithfully the luck of its beginnings, by acknowledging both the drive and the impossibility to know our lives, or to be ignorant of them. I think we are wrongly hopeful to speak of poetry as a kind of knowledge, and that we may be hoping for the wrong thing. It would be better, I imagine, to think of poetry as a kind of passionate and structured ignorance, like a dream.

(1983)

Wagoner, Hugo, and Levine

In Broken Country is the eleventh book of poems for David Wagoner, who has also given us nine novels. Added to this prodigious output, his wide-ranging mastery of verse forms makes him, among the important poets of his generation, the one whose authority is hardest to describe succinctly. He has so many convincing modes that his authority itself makes a reader recognize a Wagoner poem, rather than a characteristic look of the poem on the page, or verse form, or diction or subject matter. Like Roethke's other best students, he has made poetry a calling. He has relied less on poetic personality—in fact, he's made himself a chameleon—and more on his poetry than any of his few peers.

His new book includes sixty-three poems so various that if anyone else wrote them, the book would have all the formal coherence of an overfull laundry bag. But two faiths draw the book to exact shape.

Wagoner's achieved faith is that none of the behavior of language is accidental; here he applies to English itself what Freud argued for human behavior, and primarily for linguistic behavior, in *The Psychopathology of Everyday Life*. Puns, clichés, rhymes, rhythmic and metrical patterns are all valuable to the poet, because their significances are historical and communal; his own discoveries may be only idiosyncratic. Here whatever of style is personality is given away and a chastening taken up.

The faith that Wagoner has been given is an obsessive body of subject matter: Indiana, music and music lessons, fundamentalist Christianity, the laws and exceptions from laws of nature in relation to the laws and exceptions from laws of language, Washington, Roethke's influence and example, Northwest American Indians, hunting and trapping and logging, love and its disciplines, the self and its disciplines.

The first of *In Broken Country*'s three sections begins in boyhood—landscape, music lessons, church—and moves to a group of remarkable love poems that are like charms or prayers ("For a Woman Who Said Her Soul Was Lost" and "For a Woman Who Dreamed All the Horses Were Dying" are two titles). That section also includes the following poem, "The Singers," which bears an epigraph from Mathilde Marchesi's *Correct Methods of Vocal Study*: "Lend no ear to those that advise you to practice with a smile. It becomes set, and one never gets rid of it."

> Others may smile and smile, forgetting to try
> To smile but always smiling, at our service,
> The comic masks running and running for office,
> Or those running from office to office, their lips
> Turned up at the busy corners, or the speechless lovers
> Smiling at fortune, even the ballerina
> Persuading us her labors are pure joy,
> All beamed by the glistening skin of their teeth
> Hopefully into a climate of agreement.
>
> But not the singers. Without false promises,
> Leaving their smiles for later, lifting their voices
> With calm, straight faces, they must face their music.

The "skin of their teeth" and "must face their music" are two buried metaphors Wagoner exhumes here, and also at graveside he finds something from *Hamlet*: "others may smile and smile." The poem is a remarkable contest between anger and accuracy. It seems to me deeply Protestant—*work,* it urges through skinned teeth, *not faith.* Reading about these hymn-singers, I felt the urgency and ferocity of the Reformation. And a central clash in Wagoner's imagination is in the poem. What is it like to answer a calling? The calling never wants whom it calls, but only something he might have. How much does art make the self, and how much does art ask to have the self returned, like an emptied bottle? Capacities analogous to the poet's are crucial to the dramatic situations of poems in this section: librarian, public speaker, actor, the boy Jesus (ironically, the poem's speaker is an actor in a school pageant who finally invests his "fidgety faith" in his own words), a musician, a player-piano (a kind of midwestern Aeolian harp), sorcerer's apprentice, stonemason, builder of model airplanes (Icarus and Boeing both), singer, missing singer, choir director, gardener, and rose.

If the gardener's role is work and the rose's is faith—both in the gardener and in the rose's own genetic imperative to thrive no matter how well or poorly the gardener performs, but then finally dependent on that performance—then we can see how unified an obsession Wagoner has invested in these apparently occasional and unrelated poems.

The boyhood potentials of the first section of *In Broken Country* are at range in the second section. The field is ethical and the proof of seriousness peril:

> This rubble, pitched and jackstrawed to the horizon,
> Was a forest deep enough to be lost in,

says a poem on a clear-cut forest, and for Wagoner to be "lost" means that the possibility of real discovery—he will find the true world, or it him—is gained. The exigencies of being human are at times part of the problem, at times part of the solution, and usually both.

> I wait my turn, a man grown desperate to be grown,
> To be filled, to be fulfilled before it's too late
> Even to hope for a sign from barn swallows, these masters
> Of aimless, unpremeditated, single-minded grace, now flying
> Carelessly through barbed wire, diving and doubling . . .

"Carelessly . . . diving and doubling" sound wonderful, especially after the rigors of "single-minded grace"; if only we were birds. Or, as Roethke had it, "I would with the fish. . . ."

The third section of *In Broken Country* is Wagoner's version of Roethke's "North American Sequence," both homage and declaration of independence.

Homage: Roethke gave us a sense that the life of the self—that's too small a word—or the spirit—is happening before our eyes, present participial. Wagoner has twelve poems in this section, eleven of them with present participles in their titles.

Declaration of independence: For Roethke, the landscape comprised a possible vocabulary for the spirit (Pound: "the natural object is always the adequate symbol"). For Wagoner, the object is a strict correction to the self (Wagoner: "Your rope with nothing at the end of it / But the end of it"), and without such corrections, the self can seem spiritless.

The book's title comes from this section. "In this broken country / the shortest distance between two points doesn't exist." Here the desert sand "takes you as you are, dead or alive / As a kind of minor natural disaster." And while the overwhelming impression these poems give is of the landscape's resistance to the humans who so little deserve the landscape's harsh bounties, connections are possible between man and land, e.g., "Young trees lean *with* you / Like the new grass in this clearing where you've stumbled" (Wagoner's italics).

It would be best for this desert if no human ever went there. But we go there because it is, as Wagoner tells us, the best, most chastising, and most necessary landscape to us.

For all the ablutions it is asked, in the dry West, to perform; for all it is asked to evaporate of pathetic fallacy; for all Wagoner gives it to us as the thing itself . . . Finally, for and despite all these assignments, this broken country *is* the imagination, the West to which, on good and life-filling advice, the young man went. And where, still, he meditates on the breadth of human responsibility and the limits of human power.

That meditation throws Wagoner again and again (his poems are a cycle more than a sequence) toward conflicting urges. One is theological, to love the sinner and despise the sin (when the sinner is the Weyerhauser Company, Wagoner finds this impossible). The other is psychological, to internalize both the sin and the sinner and thus be unbroken. The last poem in Wagoner's cycle defines, having come this far, starting over.

The life in your hands is neither here nor there
But getting there,
So you're standing again and breathing, beginning another
Journey without regret
Forever, being your own unpeaceable kingdom,
The end of endings.

"*In Broken Country* is one more solid book in the literary trail of a man who keeps our desire for independence alive and makes us less reluctant to accept ourselves," writes Richard Hugo in his blurb for a fellow student of Roethke, and he's right. The writing of blurbs is so exact and demanding a literary form that it invariably reveals more about the blurber than the blurbee, and on that score Hugo has told us much about his own work, in which reluctance to accept ourselves is a pulse, and independence is not only the nourishing and normal solitude of being human but also a terrifying and uncontrolled secession from the human community. And how, if we are torn like that, can we accept ourselves? How would we begin?

Long-time admirers of Hugo's work have sensed how seriously this was the knot at the heart of it, and his *Selected Poems* are confirmation. At the core of his diction we find verbs like *degrade, shame, humiliate,* and nouns like *home,* adjectives like *good,* adverbs like *easily.* As a religious man who knows his sect's secret name for God seldom uses it in prayers, Hugo seldom says *accept* or *acceptance* in his poems but can barely write a blurb—and he's generous with them—without implicitly defining poetry as that which makes us want to take ourselves on.

It's wonderful to have the poems from Hugo's first three books—now out of print—available again. Behind the lines we can hear the cadence Roethke took "from a man named Yeats," but we can hear, too, from the beginning, the booming monosyllables and syntax so folksy and working-class on one level that we need time to hear how sophisticatedly askew it is on another level. And in these earliest poems we can see how these levels would be thoroughly welded when Hugo grew, as the momentum and force of his rhythms suggested he would, relentless.

Hugo has used towns to embody community and social organization, enemies of independence, and tokens of acceptance. Triggering towns, we've learned to call them from his *The Triggering Town: Lectures and Essays on Poetry and Writing* (1979). He means strange towns about which one knows little or nothing, and which one can therefore use as a series of screens on which to objectify the same (essentially) but ever-different (in detail) contest between self-acceptance and self-condemnation.

In "La Push" (from *A Run of Jacks*—salmon, not playing cards—1961) he begins:

> Fish swim onto sand in error.
> Birds need only the usual wind
> to be fanatic, no bright orange
> or strange names. Waves fall
> from what had been flat water,
> and a child sells herring
> crudely at your door.

The high percentage of stressed syllables, the stout stanzas with lines of regular length, the internal rhymes and few end rhymes, the leaps in association more disjunctive than the grammatical or syntactical indications of "leaps" would suggest, the preponderance of short words (only *fanatic* and *usual* exceed two syllables), the assertive and confident tone are all there—less flexible and idiosyncratic, both, than now, but there. Also the love of fish, towns, children getting tact wrong, sameness and grayness vs. bright and strange, and water as a force that herds both rejection and acceptance, water that in its currency, its rise and fall, sweeps uniformly away what would be opposites in an unmoving logic. Also, La Push is a scruffy town on the Washington coast from which commercial salmon-fishing expeditions set out with tourists, the sort of town Hugo can find in Montana or Italy or Washington, or, given the opportunity, in Nicaragua, since he carries it with him everywhere. Also, the end rhymes are not so few as we first think (*error/water/door*: a characteristic trio for Hugo), nor the metrics so irregular, nor is the diction without an almost disclaimed sophistication (note how *error, fanatic, flat* and *crudely* combine to define by implication, a certain failure of vision).

Also important to Hugo from the beginning—as to Wagoner and Levine—is the seldom explicit but haunting theme of class in American life, a topic on which we have arranged to have little intelligent discussion by asserting loudly that we are a classless society, or at least one with great mobility between classes. Both assertions are wrong. "You a gentleman and I up from the grime," one poem begins. This is the grime of degradation, which in Hugo's work we're likely—it seems to comfort us—to talk about in psychological terms, but it is also, of course, the grime of dull work and discomfort and poverty, the dirt that means you work with your hands and maybe not by choice.

Hugo's selections for this volume ought to provide readers with full collections of his work a chance to ask themselves why their favorite poems weren't included. One could quibble here and there, but no poem central to Hugo's work is left out.

Since *Selected Poems* came out, a new collection has appeared, *White Center*, the title not only a rich metaphor but also the name of a lower-working-class section of West Seattle where Hugo grew up. "He is the man I would have become," Hugo says of a heartsick and defeated man in the White Center he goes back to see.

> I want
> to tell him I've been writing poems
> the long time I've been away and need
> to compare them with poems
> I left here, never to be written, never
> to be found in the attic where hornets
> starve and there's no flooring.

The book is haunted by that sad man.

> I can't let it go, the picture I keep of myself
> in ruin, living alone, some wretched town
> where friendship is based on just being around.

150

But, explicitly in the poem "Leaving the Dream" and implicitly throughout *White Center*, Hugo insists that the sad man is not Hugo. I think the sad man represents the delusions of hope, and that a crucial imaginative struggle in *White Center* is that between the personal hopefulness necessary not to live in ruin, alone, just being around, on the one hand, and on the other, the lures and ruths of hope. Here is "Brief History."

> Dust was too thick every summer. Every winter
> at least one animal died, a good friend,
> and we forgot the burial ritual after our Bible
> washed away in the flood. We mumbled anything
> that occurred to us over the grave. Finally
> only our wives were left to hate, our children
> who ran off to Detroit and never came back.
> How we raged at change, the year the ground
> went fallow, the time our wheat grew purple
> and the government couldn't explain. Less fish
> in the lake every year, grain prices falling
> and falling through dark air, the suicide bird
> who showed us the good way out. The century
> turned without celebration. We tried to find fun
> in the calendar, the strange new number, nineteen.
> It was women held us together. They cautioned
> us calm the day we shouted we knew
> where millions in diamonds were buried
> and ran at the cattle swinging the ax.
> We forget that now. We are planning hard
> for the century ahead.

It is almost as if Hugo were asking himself, again and again, how he can warn against hope without giving up hope. In his "Degrees of Gray in Philipsburg," from *The Lady in Kicking Horse Reservoir* (1973), Hugo imagines towns of visionary comforts, towns

> of towering blondes, good jazz and booze
> the world will never let you have
> until the town you come from dies inside.

But if he should hope for that Heavenly City of Salesmen, he would need to kill White Center and his own white center, and he would need to leave the working class and join the traveling class, who act out their hope for social mobility by restlessness. He would replace that grime by whiteness. And yet if he should not hope to leave White Center, then he might become, for all his protestations, the sad man there, loyal to his ruinous past, growing grime like a mold.

I see no way out of this dilemma when it's stated this way, and neither does great-hearted Hugo. History suggests how much we live by wrong hope, and poetry tells us how much we die without hope, and, too, die by failing to distrust it. How wonderfully and frighteningly Hugo struggles with this crux; how much—this too is frightening—we need his inability to trust himself, or to trust us.

Philip Levine's *Ashes* is a miraculous amalgamation of new and old poems. While Wagoner has a collected poems through 1976 (Indiana University Press) and Hugo a selected poems, we'll have to wait, in Levine's case, until he huddles with Atheneum's Harry Ford, his exemplary editor, to have in one book a large view of his continuous achievement. But this book serves as a hint. Half the poems are from *Red Dust,* published by George Hitchcock's kayak press in 1971 and long out of print, and half are recent. Without checking my copy of *Red Dust* or the copyright page of *Ashes,* I couldn't surely place poems in either group, since Levine's work is so obsessive, consistently good, and continuous. And yet, once you know which are which, you can see the improvement, the steady development.

All his work does seem to be one body, one thing. Or a dust or oil or ash that comes from one thing being used up, or many things being used up so that they reduce themselves to one thing. "The long line of diesels" is the book's first line, and the book describes throughout the world using itself up to go on being the world.

Some of the poems are set in Spain, which turns out to have a palpable connection to Fresno, where Levine has lived so long:

> . . . red dust, that dust which
> even here I taste, having eaten it
> all these years.

It's the dust of work, of getting up and going to work, eating
work in order to eat dinner, and how the world doesn't care
about and is poorly served by the endless frictions of our
survival. Here's the beginning stanza of "Fists" (1971).

> Iron growing in the dark,
> it dreams all night long
> and will not work. A flower
> that hates God, a child
> tearing at itself, this one
> closes on nothing.

It's matter itself, the fool's gold of industrial life, that resists
industrial life, sated and smug and glowing and lazy (*pig iron*,
it's called in one of its manifestations); it's as if matter fed *us* to
the refining fires. Hence the title, *Ashes*.

That time is irrecoverable is a powerful urge in lyric poetry,
but Levine's fascination with work results in a sense of time
different from that in most lyric poetry. Many of his poems
are about waking up, the long day, the world sped along by
the relentlessness of time but the job, somehow, both hero-
ically and stupidly, remaining the same. "We are the dignified
/ by dirt," Levine says in "Making It New," not out of a Stein-
beckian sentimentality for numbing work, but because he sees
work to be quixotic, a kind of biological joke we become hu-
man by playing on ourselves, and thereby join the rest of the
world we might otherwise hold ourselves wrongly above—
grasses, gulls, ores, and debris.

There's something degrading, to borrow a trope from Hu-
go, about all this dirty dignity, and that may explain the splen-
did truculence in Levine's poems. A poem called "Father" ends

> I find you
> in these tears, few
> useless and here at last.
>
> Don't come back.

If the inheritance is this drab and usual response to time—
working to make ashes—then, say the heirs, to hell with it and
don't come back. What an elegy!

And there are these lines from "Starlight," a poem about a
father and a son.

> He has found nothing, and he smiles
> and holds my head with both his hands.
> Then he lifts me to his shoulder,
> and now I too am there among the stars,
> as tall as he. Are you happy? I say.
> He nods in answer, Yes! oh yes! oh yes!
> And in that new voice he says nothing,
> holding my head tight against his head,
> his eyes closed against the starlight,
> as though those tiny blinking eyes
> of light might find a tall, gaunt child
> holding his child against the promises
> of autumn, until the boy slept
> never to waken in that world again.

How rapidly Levine can move, the way our inner lives move,
from truculence to tenderness, and back, and back and forth.

What are the ashes? Cinders from industry, the ashes of the
dead, trees that will be burned, the footnotes of fire.

Behind David Wagoner's poems we can sense the sky above
Gary, Indiana, glowing, and behind Richard Hugo's poems
we can hear the dust being pushed from one part of White
Center to another. For Levine it's his native Detroit that he
carries everywhere, like an urn of ashes. The second stanza of
"Fists" reads

> Friday, late,
> Detroit Transmission. If I live
> forever, the first clouded light
> of dawn will flood me
> in the cold streams
> north of Pontiac.

Endurance is his theme, as reconciliation is Wagoner's and
acceptance is Hugo's. How do we live, our best poetry begins

by asking, and ends—though none of these poets is near an end, all three in their fifties only—by telling us how we get by. Here is the third and final stanza of "Fists."

> It opens and is no longer.
> Bud of anger, kinked
> tendril of my life, here
> in the forged morning
> fill with anything—water,
> light, blood, but fill.

Concurrent with *Ashes,* Atheneum published *7 Years from Somewhere,* a book consisting entirely of new poems. The problems of matching the *Red Dust* poems to newer poems in *Ashes* have been well solved, but they make the book less various than its companion.

There is a story famous in poetry circles about one of Levine's readings—so famous that it doubtless bears no resemblance to what actually happened. In the middle of a reading Levine looked up at his audience and confessed that this wasn't his real face, he was wearing a mask. And he reached up and grabbed his face with his hands, and his face was so plastic and mobile (I picture a thin Buddy Hackett) that he almost convinced his audience he was twisting a mask from his face. The story ends there, and what I've always wanted to know is how reader and audience regathered themselves to go on.

The Levine of that anecdote is more visible in *7 Years from Somewhere,* which begins with a poem called "I Could Believe."

> I could come to believe
> almost anything, even
> my soul, which is
> my unlit cigar, even
> the earth that huddled
> all these years to
> my bones, waiting
> for the little of me
> it would claim. . . .

And later in the poem the speaker could believe this:

and my mother would
climb into the stars
hand over hand,
a woman of imagination
and stamina among
the airy spaces
of broken clouds,
and I, middle-aged
and heavy, would
buy my suits by
the dozen, vested ones,
and wear a watch chain
stretched across my
middle. . . .

And fifty-eight lines later the speaker ends

except
for the dying I could
believe.

Another poem begins "I did not know your life / was mine," and another "Let me begin again as a speck." The range of rhetorical and dramatic situations Levine finds for himself in these poems is important, since the relentlessness of time and work, his beloved subjects, could induce in him a relentlessness of poetic means. That unswerving confrontation is practically his hallmark, of course, but who among the few poets as accomplished as those I've considered in this brief review isn't fearful of his strengths? I'll end by quoting the third and final stanza of "In the Dark."

Once, as a boy, I
climbed the attic stairs
in a sleeping house
and entered a room
no one used. I found
a trunk full of letters
and postcards from a man
who had traveled for years
and then come home to die.

In moonlight each one
said the same thing: how
long the nights were, how
cold it was so far away
and how it had to end.

(1981)

Travel

In Siena I tugged a drawer in my hotel room and it slid toward me with that smooth rumble that means good cabinet-making. Empty. There's a Truffaut film (*La Peau Douce?*) in which a traveler headed for an assignation strides into his hotel room and one by one switches on every light, as if he were filling the blank dark of the hotel room with the glare of his own fantasy life. The erotics of travel, with their powerful undertow of melancholy, are most intense in a good hotel room. Lovely, one thinks, but something's missing. Could it be me? I began to fill the drawers. I would be there four nights.

Six in the evening. Haze hung in the burnishing light like a scrim. From one window I could see the glittering pool and from the other birds swirling and darting above the juts and slopes of the town's tiled roofs, a whole landscape in themselves. Time to shower, time to sit in the garden and wait for dinner, as if for an assignation.

In the morning I'll set out to find a place where I can sit outdoors, sip a cappuccino and read the *Herald Tribune*. The farther you are from home, the shorter the articles in the newspapers available in your native language. A line score stands for a whole baseball game, and in six lines from Reuters hundreds die in a plane crash. My father loves travel and loves to read of transportation disasters. He's lived for years in England, unrepentantly American. Once, he told me, he sat outdoors on a warm spring day in London with a milk shake, a rare treat, and read contentedly about a plane crash at Tenerife. "I was," he said, "about as happy as one can be." To travel is to engage the fantasy that one can be at home anywhere, though Rimbaud wrote home from Ethiopa, "What am I doing here?" But, turning the pages of the *Herald Tribune*, I'll know what my father meant. One is like a tic on the flank of a huge and, for now, hospitable animal. Somewhere else, hundreds of tics may perish, but here? Mmmm. Warm fur. Good blood.

✖

"The word travel is the same as the French *travail*," writes Bruce Chatwin. "It means hard work, penance and finally a journey."

✖

One morning we were aloft by seven and flew in a hot-air balloon over San Gimignano, counting the famous towers. Thirteen. Everywhere in Tuscany you can see the hills rising from the rolling land to the walled towns, like clenched fists. In the thirteenth century San Gimignano fought off barbarian invaders, as non-Tuscan hostile forces were called, and also fought their neighbors: Poggibonsi, Volterra, Colle Val d'Elsa. In 1300 Dante went to San Gimignano to make a speech urging the unity of all the Guelph cities in Tuscany. They went on fighting each other. By 1301 Dante was exiled from Florence for life.

But you have to struggle to think of such things in a balloon. Fully inflated, ours were a hundred feet high and seventy feet wide. You could be dangling from a flying building. You're traveling with the wind, so you can't hear it, and pass through a preternatural calm above one of the most beautiful landscapes on earth. One of the three burners emits a frequency humans can't hear, but which drives dogs crazy. Everything is calm and beautiful and seen from a distance, and below the dogs snarl and twist and yelp.

Back on the ground, in San Gimignano, you can stare up at the towers. They were often built in pairs, joined at the tops by wooden bridges. These are long gone. For the great families in San Gimignano fought each other. The towers were not, like the giraffe's head in the savannah, the high outpost of watchfulness over the countryside but brooding emblems of vanity and hatred. You climbed as high as you could go in one of your towers or the other, and when someone tried to come up, you killed him.

Of course now the town is as famous for its towers as it is for Vernaccia, its crisp white wine, and for Ghirlandaio's fresco of the Annunciation in the cathedral. It can all become part of a mesmerizing wash of sensations, which you float somewhat through but mostly over.

I value my hours in the balloon. But finally to travel not through a benign daze but by your own curiosity and with some love for the emotional life of the place you're passing through, you have to brood long on those dogs.

We're straggling along the Autostrade in the slow lane. The BMWs and Volvos swirl by at 160 kilometers per hour. Now and then a Maserati growls past even faster, and in our rented Fiat Panda we feel more and more like passengers on a roller skate with delusions of grandeur.

"Who lives in Gubbio?" A. asks.

"Gubbians," I tell her.

Here's a tiny mystery for which I'm sure there's an easy solution, but I can't find it. Once I quoted a nostrum to a friend, who liked it. "Where's it from?" he asked.

"It's from the Confucian Analects," I said authoritatively, because I thought it was.

Later, when he was interested in finding it to use it as an epigram in a book, he couldn't find it in the Analects and neither could I.

The mystery isn't where I found it, or whether I made it up. If I could say what the mystery is it wouldn't be a mystery. I think mystery may be too grand a word for it. Go on too long or too grandly about anything and it becomes silly. No doubt that's why I'm addicted to writing poems, with their illusory endings. But I think their silences are like the self-deceptions by which we live.

Here's the nostrum. "The way out is through the door. How is it nobody remembers this method?"

✕

The day before San Gimignano we landed in a field to the east of Siena, and as we came down the balloon's shadow startled a small herd of goats. We also flushed from cover behind a windbreak of poplars two middle-aged lovers who had somehow made it to the outskirts of town, undressed in a tiny Fiat little bigger than a bathtub, seen a balloon drift silently down from above, dressed frantically, and spurted back toward Siena dragging a rooster tail of dust along the unpaved road—all before 8:30 A.M. Then busloads of Italian army parachutists came roaring through the dust the other way to use the field for calisthenics and maneuvers. The officers wandered over to see what we were up to and wound up helping us deflate the balloon, roll up the envelope, and stuff it back into the chase van. We offered them *spumante* but they were on duty. They gave us chocolate in dun-colored government wrappers—dark, intense, wonderful bittersweet chocolate. The field was formerly an airstrip, the biggest open space for miles around. Balloonists love open spaces and hate power lines. "You hit a power line," A. loved to say, "you're toast."

✕

Every family is a conspiracy of heartbreak, and thus a family traveling together becomes a small band of smugglers. You wait and wait. One of you smokes and another of you hates it. The people who go by probably belong here and have ordinary lives. Then the train stutters and rolls off. Customs agents pass through the train like a combine through a field. Instead of a heart you have a rabbit in your chest. But it's no use. They come and go. You'll never be discovered. It will always be like this.

✕

Every morning the balloon pilot released a trial balloon, the kind you'd buy for a child at a dime store. The verdict was swift: where it went our balloon would go.

161

The day after San Gimignano we took off west of Siena and drifted over the city's heart, the Campo, the piazza shaped like a clamshell where the three hills on which the city has been built meet. In the Campo dirt was being laid for the Palio.

Siena is divided into seventeen *contrade* (an exact translation would be a word that occupies a space equidistant from "parish" and "precinct"). Each has a name, colors, a budget for running the Palio, and a master strategist.

The Palio is a bareback horserace, two and a half laps around the periphery of the Campo. The race is run July 2 and August 16. Ten *contrade* compete, so each race includes the seven excluded from the last race and three chosen by lot.

There are no rules of good conduct for the race. Horses are assigned by lot, but a *contrada* must buy the services of a jockey. There's room and board for the horse, naturally, and what's left in the budget goes for bribes.

It's best to win, but worst that your enemies win. It's widely assumed that most bribes are tendered in hopes of insuring another *contrada*'s defeat, but since bribes are by nature *sub rosa,* who knows?

Before the race each *contrada* blesses its horse, led in colors to the altar.

A balloon is as close as a human gets to know how a cloud feels. We tufted languidly over the city. Below us—please don't photograph the prisonyard—deals were struck over coffee.

A *contrada* is usually named for conventionally impressive animals (eagle, panther) but there's a caterpillar, too, and it hasn't won in thirty-seven years. The silks and banners of each *contrada* are sumptuous. The long, fevered wars between the city-states are rehearsed here, and the vitriolic isolations of the towertops, and by such flurry some pilot light is tended that can ignite in any of us the sanctimonies of home and thus the need to travel.

To dawdle is at the center of travel. To eat outdoors on a warm night in Rome, let's say, and linger over the last of the wine is not only to soak in one's own pleasure, as in a tub, but to live out the open secret of pleasure: it spites time. Good meals last long. The purpose of sexual intercourse is to get it over with as slowly as possible. The function of rhythm in poetry is to manipulate time, to prefer rather than the steady onslaught of actuarial time, 4,200 heartbeats per hour, the lulled trance in which good poems insist that they be read.

Ours is an age that measures time most accurately by the rate of decay of radioactive matter. This method is not only an improvement over the methods of earlier ages, but also a convulsive embrace of a powerful metaphor. There are arts that happen in "real time," like music and film, and part of their authority for heartbreak is that they do. Poetry refers by its every formal wile to our urge to go more slowly, and that longing is part of poetry's authority for heartbreak. Travel is like that. You walk for a while. You sit there and sip. You stand there and look.

✂

Is travel, whatever else it is, a kind of narrative, a picaresque, I suppose? How did W.M., a small-town boy with a smattering of Latin, get to Orvieto on this particular sweat-drenched afternoon?

Probably travel is not the path of explanation and causality, but, whatever else it is, the path by which we act out an impossible longing for explanation and causality. The dog of emotional life, narrative comes ever at the heels of experience.

✂

The early raptures of reading are the first travel.

But what if I should go back to Troy, Ohio, and retrace the path I rode and rerode on my bike, to and from the public library? Back at the old house the sentinel hollyhocks, with their dusty carillons, no longer grow against the toolshed.

How much of the work of leaving Troy was done by reading. Leaning against the base of that tree, and in that high window, the work of rupture was slowly and stubbornly performed in the silent thrall of reading.

So that when I finally left I took with me as much of what I had learned from reading to love, even my sorrow. No wonder this small county seat looks freshly cleaned, as if for company. I look down McKaig Avenue past the porched white

163

houses toward the pebbled playground infield that surely is still but three minutes fevered ride away.

To love this place again as I did then I'd need to reinvent it, and in order to leave again reinvent the travail, the working through, the penance.

※

Florence is hot and saturated with tourists. The youngest of them, college age, carry plastic bottles of Evian water and trade travel tips: "The lines are shortest at the Uffizi at lunchtime." Older tourists are distractedly sweeping the Via Tournaboni, it seems, for one last leather good. I can feel a distasteful sourness building in me that I recognize, not happily, as a traveler's greed and fatigue akin to the teacher's pleasure in walking across campus on vacation, when the students are all gone.

The Boboli Gardens are cool and people sparse there. I wander around the gardens for two hours and then head back to my air-conditioned hotel room. It's a day when the active, animal alertness of travel just wants a day off. OK. I switch on the TV to see if there's any coverage of Wimbledon and see that the Palio is being telecast.

They've been running the race since 1656. The ten horses are tensed between the two restraining ropes. The front rope goes slack and in ninety seconds it's over. Three jockeys are thrown; two horses go down. The winning *contrada* is La Selva (the forest), named for something that can't move. It must have come straight from the Latin *silva*, I think idly. The TV is showing reruns of the race, but I'm no longer watching. I sit in a cool room sipping a glass of Prosecco from the frigobar, shut off from and yet in thrall to the vast world, *silva rerum,* the forest of things.

※

From a letter from S.M.: "Travel is, for me, the most beautiful intoxicant. The words of travel, *valise,* for example; what couldn't you pack into that? Where couldn't you take it?"

Where couldn't you take it? We travel in order to find out.

(1988)

A Poet's Alphabet

A poet is "too close" to an impulse or obsession; what he needs from it is aesthetic distance. Notice that this prescription prefers to the poem the poet is struggling to write, a poem the physician believes the poet ought to write, but later. Aesthetic distance is usually about feeling superior to emotional life and contains a built-in reason for not asking why. What we need is aesthetic intimacy.

"Aesthetics is for the artist," said the painter and sculptor Barnett Newman, "like ornithology is for the birds."

There is a great and cruel pun in the metaphor of the corpus, the body of work, for it grows compensatingly larger and more capable as the poet's own body grows stiffer and less resilient. Of course, the latter happens in any case.

Criticism has a separate role, though perhaps a smaller one than is usually supposed, in the study of literature; it is like the role of anatomy in the study of medicine. "Anatomy presupposes a corpse," D'Annunzio observed. A critic is interested in completed work, and a poet in the work he is just now doing or just about to do. One is a student of literature, the other is practicing it.

Dreams resemble poems in their crucial mechanisms: compression, condensation, preference for metaphor to simile, and in how little time they take. And in the *Interpretation of Dreams*, Freud notes that every dream wholly resists interpretation at some declivity, that it has an umbilical connection to what is knowable; good poems are like this. Interestingly, transcribed dreams make bad poems. For a poem, an Italian critic once said, is "a dream dreamed in the presence of reason."

✕

In Po Biz, as Louis Simpson snappishly called it, where rewards and honors are comparatively few and small, there can be vast envy. Nobody fights for food when the platter is full. So praise where you honestly can, lest our provisions dwindle.

✕

"The ants set an example to us all," wrote Max Beerbohm, "but it is not a good one."

✕

One writes for a number of reasons, but the best and most terrifying is freedom. For when a poet's imagination is working at full capacity, he can only be coerced by himself.

✕

"G" is for grant money, for prizes, for all the tiny blares, briefer than flashbulbs, of public recognition. We all know, or seem to, because we all say it, that the processes that produce these honors are "political," as if almost every human activity involving two or more people weren't political, by our very natures. It is good policy not to assail the corrupt and craven people who fail one year to give you an honor, for next year the louts may give it to you and you will have spoiled your small fun in advance.

✕

Happiness is not wholly an accident, some prosperous suburb of luck. We create our work, and the work changes us. It not only describes to those who can read the signs some path we have traveled, but it contains, too, some element of prophesy. Finally the reason we should make our work the best we can is not an abstraction like pride or character, but the very concrete likelihood that we will become, somehow, the persons whom our work has made possible. There is of course something in us wholly obdurate and truculent, something the work can't change at all. I have no idea what the proportion is between the two.

✖

"Incompetence consists of wanting to reach conclusions," said Flaubert. And in fear of incompetence. To write well, wrote Joubert, "one needs a natural facility and an acquired difficulty."

✖

"J" is for jazz. When Pound demanded that the poet write "in the sequence of the musical phrase, rather than of the metronome," he might have been predicting Lester Young. Nobody could have predicted Louis Armstrong or Charlie Parker. Much of the nonsense spoken in the debate over traditional vs. free verse could be avoided, I like to think, by inciting the combatants to learn a little jazz history. I'd concentrate on the late years of swing and the early years of bop, when improvisation on the melody and the blue notes in a scale gave way to improvisation on the chord changes of a song. Why is it that masterful musicians like Coleman Hawkins and Roy Eldridge were able to play well in both idioms? Because they understood that while each idiom suppressed certain rhythmic effects in order to favor others, the possibility in each case was rhythm, the structuring of emotion in time.

"J" is also for jokes, with their energy compressed, stored, then released. Like springs. And for how much jokes are about language, about misunderstanding, anxiety, ambiguous tone.

To tell jokes well, any good comedian will say, you have to pay exact attention to timing.

✖

Knowledge gets opposed to experience in much talk about poetry, but in fact, human consciousness is so composed that

167

we can't have experience without a commentary on it. This makes us both silly and interesting. It makes us want to bring out apparently disparate perceptions together, to make structures that comprehend what might on first or lazy thought— or first or lazy feeling—seem finally separate. It makes us want to make poems.

✕

"L" is for limitations, and how artists wrench them into strengths.

An aristocratic British flier shot down an aristocratic German flier, according to the rules of war, and then according to the rules of aristocracy he went to visit him in the hospital. "Can I do anything for you?" he asked. *Noblesse oblige.*

"Actually," the German pilot said, "there is one thing. I was rather banged up in the crash, and the doctors have had to amputate a leg to keep me alive. I wonder if you'd be willing to take it with you on your next bombing run and drop it over the Fatherland."

An odd request, but he did it, and then went back to the hospital to say he had.

"I'm sorry to trouble you again," the German pilot began, "but I've taken a turn for the worse and they've sawed off my other leg. I wonder if, er. . . ."

"Consider it done," said the British pilot, and he did, and then came back to report.

"I'm sorry to prevail upon you one more time," the German pilot said. "But they've had to take off an arm."

The British pilot didn't like this at all, but *noblesse oblige.* He was leaving the hospital room with the German's arm under his arm when a thought struck him. "I say, old boy, you wouldn't be trying to escape, would you?"

✕

Memory is a constant goad to writing. But memory is not a system of information storage and retrieval. Memory itself is a kind of writing.

✕

Nostalgia is memory as narcosis. The problem with the past is that the older we are, the more there is of it. It can seem like life's work to a poet, but if he should take it on, the life begins to be at the mercy of that work.

✗

Croesus needed to know if he should attack Cyrus of Persia, and so consulted the Delphic oracle. "Attack him and a great empire will fall." He attacked and the lost empire was his own. Oracular language hedges its bets, has it both ways, and invites the listener or reader to find in deliberate ambiguity what the listener or reader wants to find there. In poetry it is almost always the result of failure to be responsible to clarity, and often the result of scheming to look knowing.

✗

Prosody is hard to talk about because it gets confused with other subjects. *Free verse* sounds like "Free Huey!" The confusion between poetry and politics is endemic. William Carlos Williams, who should have known better, once said that the sonnet is a fascist form because it made the words run on time. And Frost should have known better than that sleazily easy joke about playing tennis with the net down. Surely it's hard to know if, in politics, our century has suffered more from too much or too little order. If we could talk about the behavior of language in poems rather than about how to get poems to engender the political values we espouse (such talk is not about behavior but about behavior modification), we might restore prosody to the interesting topic it should be.

✗

"Q" is for quiet. A poem is both an organization of sounds and an organization of silences. Silence is the great, inaudible dial tone that both threatens poetry and makes it possible.

✗

It would be better if we did not think, in seeking publication for our poems, of rejection. Or of submission, for that matter. The diction itself gives to editors and publishers a wrong

169

power, which only the best of them don't want. Isn't it really a business transaction? "Would you like these poems? Yes or no?"

※

Subject matter is the occasion of speech in a poem, quite literally a pretext. If a poem should linger where it begins, how could it be called "moving"?

※

"Three impossible things," Freud listed: to teach, to govern, to cure.

It is because translation is impossible that it's interesting.

※

Universities house and feed so many poets that we are likely to resent them the way artists earlier resented patrons. "Is not a Patron, my Lord, one who looks on a man struggling for life in the water, and, when he has reached ground, encumbers him with help?" Samuel Johnson wrote to Lord Chesterfield. But it should not be shocking that two parties to a contract or a relationship want different things from it. We could describe our ties to publishers and lovers this way, and yet we publish and love persistently. It must be that we need to negotiate well.

※

"Now," proclaims a critic, "So-and-so has finally found his voice." How can this be? His voice was surely found where it's been all along, in his throat. In fact, as we know, voices are as unique as fingerprints. Surely what our critic is struggling to describe is that moment when a younger poet ceases to contribute his voice wholly to choral subject matter and begins to speak not as a ventriloquist for the tribe or *zeitgeist,* but for his mortal self.

※

The very name "workshop" suggests the Calvinist vocabulary and community values that workshops too often prefer. "Does it work?" "Did the poets earn those last lines?" Thus poems are weighed in the scales. Interestingly enough, the most valuable thing learned in cumbersome workshops is neither earnest nor communal, but how crucial play is to the work of writing.

Against writing programs it is argued that they encourage sameness in their students, and that bad poems proliferate thereby. In fact writing programs themselves are said, with a shudder, to proliferate. Surely the underlying metaphor here is cancer, and failure to distinguish between a dull sestina and cancer is a likely signal of hysteria.

Who among us has been harmed by a bad poem, against his consent? Who among us wants to teach students so cagily cautious that they never write bad poems?

As for sameness, do not we as primates learn by imitation? A writing program brings young poets together, lets them imitate each other, squabble, learn from each other, envy and sabotage and compete with each other. It is from this moil as much as from our teaching that they learn, we should notice. And we should notice, while we're trying to be honest, that the behavior of young poets I have described above does not differ greatly from the behavior of older poets, except that it happens in a more controlled space.

"X" is for xenophobia, for the superstition that one's country, language, region, style or school or movement, and even one's sexual practice, invest one's poems with anything more than the circumstances out of which one inescapably writes. This is the poet's version of nationalism, in which smugness is exactly equal to the fear it masks. It is, because it comes finally from the self but is ascribed to a power outside the self, the deepest invitation to stupidity a poet can receive.

"Y" is for yourself.

✖

"Z" is the end, and so a small lesson in form and opportunism.

(1985)

UNDER DISCUSSION
David Lehman, General Editor
Donald Hall, Founding Editor

Volumes in the Under Discussion series collect reviews and essays about individual poets. The series is concerned with contemporary American and English poets about whom the consensus has not yet been formed and the final vote has not been taken. Titles in the series include: